TO:

_____

FROM:

_____

DATE:

_____

FAMILY
Christian Stores®

PROMISES & PRAYERS

for Women

FAMILY
Christian Stores

PROMISES & PRAYERS

for Women

Cover Design & Page Layout: Bart Dawson

ISBN-13: 978-1-58334-144-5

ISBN-10: 1-58334-144-7

Printed in the United States of America

For Women Everywhere

Table of Contents

INTRODUCTION

*Y*ou hold in your hands a book entitled *Promises and Prayers for Women.* Perhaps you received this book as a gift, or perhaps, amid the hustle and bustle of your busy life, you picked up this little book on your own. Either way, you will be blessed *if* you take the promises on these pages to heart.

This text addresses topics of particular interest to women. Each brief chapter contains Bible verses, a quotation from a noted Christian thinker, and a prayer. The ideas in each chapter are powerful reminders of God's commandments and of the joy and abundance He promises His children.

Being a godly woman in today's world is a daunting task. Never have expectations been higher, never have temptations been so plentiful, and never have demands been greater…and that's where God comes in. God stands ready, willing, and able to help you in every facet of your life *if* you ask Him.

This book is intended to remind you of the eternal promises that are found in God's Holy Word *and* of God's never-ending love for You. May these pages be a blessing to you, and may you, in turn, be a blessing to those whom God has seen fit to place along your path.

ABUNDANCE

I am come that they might have life, and that they might have it more abundantly.

—John 10:10 KJV

Now this I say, he who sows sparingly will also reap sparingly, and he who sows bountifully will also reap bountifully.

—2 Corinthians 9:6 NASB

My cup runneth over. Surely goodness and mercy shall follow me all the days of my life: and I will dwell in the house of the LORD for ever.

—Psalm 23:5-6 KJV

Misfortune pursues the sinner, but prosperity is the reward of the righteous.

—Proverbs 13:21 NIV

"For I know the plans I have for you," declares the Lord, "plans to prosper you and not to harm you, plans to give you hope and a future. Then you will call upon me and come and pray to me, and I will listen to you."

—Jeremiah 29:11-12 NIV

$\mathcal{G}$od sent His Son so that mankind might enjoy the abundant life that Jesus describes in the familiar words of John 10:10. But, God's gifts are not guaranteed; they must be claimed by those who choose to follow Christ. Today, accept God's promise of spiritual abundance. When you do, you will be eternally blessed.

Jesus intended for us to be overwhelmed by the blessings of regular days. He said it was the reason he had come: "I am come that they might have life, and that they might have it more abundantly."

—Gloria Gaither

—A PRAYER—

$\mathcal{H}$eavenly Father, thank You for the joyful, abundant life that is mine through Christ Jesus. Guide me according to Your will, and help me to be a worthy servant through all that I say and do. Give me courage, Lord, to claim the spiritual riches that You have promised, and lead me according to Your plan for my life, today and always.

—Amen

ACCEPTING CHRIST

And we have seen and testify that the Father has sent his Son to be the Savior of the world.

—1 John 4:14 NIV

For there is one God and one mediator between God and men, the man Christ Jesus, who gave himself as a ransom for all men....

—1 Timothy 2:5-6 NIV

And she shall bring forth a son, and thou shalt call his name JESUS: for he shall save his people from their sins.

—Matthew 1:21 KJV

For the Son of man is come to seek and to save that which was lost.

—Luke 19:10 KJV

For God so loved the world, that he gave his only begotten Son, that whosoever believeth in him should not perish, but have everlasting life.

—John 3:16 KJV

*G*od loves you. Period. And, God's love for you is so great that He sent His only Son to this earth to die for your sins and offer you the priceless gift of eternal life. Now, you must decide whether or not to accept God's gift. Will you ignore it or embrace it? Will you return it or neglect it? Will you accept Christ or not? The decision, of course, is yours and yours alone, and the decision has eternal consequences. Accept God's gift: Accept Christ.

The redemption, accomplished for us by our Lord Jesus Christ on the cross at Calvary, is redemption from the power of sin as well as from its guilt. Christ is able to save all who come unto God by Him.

—*Hannah Whitall Smith*

—A PRAYER—

*L*ord, I am only here on this earth for a brief while. But, You have offered me the priceless gift of eternal life through Your Son Jesus. I accept Your gift, Lord, with thanksgiving and praise. Let me share the good news of my salvation with those who need Your healing touch.

—*Amen*

ADVERSITY

When you go through deep waters and great trouble, I will be with you. When you go through the rivers of difficulty, you will not drown! When you walk through the fire of oppression, you will not be burned up; the flames will not consume you. For I am the Lord, your God....

—Isaiah 43:2-3 NLT

I tell you the truth, you will weep and mourn while the world rejoices. You will grieve, but your grief will turn to joy.

—John 16:20 NIV

Come to me, all you who are weary and burdened, and I will give you rest. Take my yoke upon you and learn from me, for I am gentle and humble in heart, and you will find rest for your souls. For my yoke is easy and my burden is light.

—Matthew 11:28-30 NIV

Be of good courage, and he shall strengthen your heart, all ye that hope in the LORD.

—Psalm 31:24 KJV

*W*omen of every generation have had experience with adversity, and this generation is no different. But, today's women face challenges that previous generations could have scarcely imagined. Thankfully, although the world continues to change, God's love remains constant. And, He remains ready to comfort and strengthen us whenever we turn to Him. Psalm 147 promises, "He heals the brokenhearted, and binds their wounds" (v. 3). When we are troubled, we must call upon God, and, in His own time and according to His own plan, He will heal us.

Often, in the midst of great problems, we stop short of the real blessing God has for us, which is a fresh vision of who He is.

—Anne Graham Lotz

—A PRAYER—

*H*eavenly Father, You are my strength and refuge. I can face the difficulties of this day because You are with me. You are my light and pathway. As I follow You, Father, I can overcome adversity just as Jesus overcame this world.

—Amen

ANGER

Now you must rid yourselves of all such things as these: anger, rage, malice....

—*Colossians 3:8 NIV*

A gentle answer turns away wrath, but a harsh word stirs up anger.

—*Proverbs 15:1 NIV*

Refrain from anger and turn from wrath; do not fret—it leads only to evil.

—*Psalm 37:8 NIV*

Do not let the sun go down on your anger, and do not give the devil an opportunity.

—*Ephesians 4:26-27 NASB*

You have heard it said, "Love your neighbor and hate your enemy." But I tell you: Love your enemies and pray for those who persecute you, that you may be sons of your Father in heaven.

—*Matthew 5:43-45 NIV*

Sometimes, anger is appropriate. Even Jesus became angry when confronted with the moneychangers in the temple. As long as you live here on earth, you will face countless opportunities to lose your temper over small, relatively insignificant events: a traffic jam, a spilled cup of coffee, an inconsiderate comment, a broken promise. When you are tempted to lose your temper over the minor inconveniences of life, don't. Turn away from anger, hatred, bitterness, and regret. Turn instead to God.

To handle yourself, use your head; to handle others, use your heart. Anger is only one letter short of danger.

—*Eleanor Roosevelt*

—A PRAYER—

Dear Lord, when I am angry, I cannot feel the peace that You intend for my life. When I am bitter, I cannot sense Your love. Heavenly Father, keep me mindful that forgiveness is Your commandment and Your will for my life. Let me turn away from anger and instead claim the spiritual abundance that You offer through the priceless gift of Your Son Jesus.

—*Amen*

21

ANXIETY

Cast all your anxiety on him because he cares for you.

—*1 Peter 5:7 NIV*

Do not be anxious about anything, but in everything, by prayer and petition, with thanksgiving, present your requests to God.

—*Philippians 4:6 NIV*

Let not your heart be troubled: ye believe in God, believe also in me.

—*John 14:1 KJV*

So, don't be anxious about tomorrow. God will take care of your tomorrow too. Live one day at a time.

—*Matthew 6:34 TLB*

Jesus turned and saw her. "Take heart, daughter," he said, "your faith has healed you." And the woman was healed from that moment.

—*Matthew 9:22 NIV*

Are you anxious? Take those anxieties to God. Are you troubled? Take your troubles to Him. Does your world seem to be trembling beneath your feet? Seek protection from the One who cannot be moved. The same God who created the universe will protect you if you ask Him...so ask Him.

*

The moment anxious thoughts invade your mind, go to the Lord in prayer. Look first to God. Then, you will see the cause of your anxiety in a whole new light.

—*Kay Arthur*

—A Prayer—

Heavenly Father, sometimes troubles and distractions preoccupy my thoughts and trouble my soul. When I am anxious, Lord, let me turn my prayers to You. When I am worried, give me faith in You. Let me live courageously, Dear God, knowing that You love me and that You will protect me, today and forever.

—*Amen*

ASKING GOD

You do not have, because you do not ask God.

—*James 4:2 NIV*

Verily, verily, I say unto you, He that believeth on me, the works that I do shall he do also; and greater works than these shall he do; because I go unto my Father. And whatsoever ye shall ask in my name, that will I do, that the Father may be glorified in the Son. If ye shall ask any thing in my name, I will do it.

—*John 14:12-14 KJV*

You did not choose me, but I chose you and appointed you to go and bear fruit—fruit that will last. Then the Father will give you whatever you ask in name.

—*John 15:16 NIV*

Ask and it will be given to you; seek and you will find; knock and the door will be opened to you. For everyone who asks receives; he who seeks finds; and to him who knocks, the door will be opened.

—*Matthew 7:7-8 NIV*

Are you a woman in need of renewal? Ask God to strengthen you. Are you troubled? Take your concerns to Him in prayer. Are you discouraged? Seek the comfort of God's promises. Do you feel trapped in a life that lacks fulfillment and joy? Ask God where He wants you to go, and then go there. In all things great and small, seek the transforming power of God's grace. He hears your prayers, and He will answer.

God insists that we ask, not because He needs to know our situation, but because we need the spiritual discipline of asking.

—*Catherine Marshall*

—A PRAYER—

Lord, You are the giver of all things good. When I am in need, let me come to You in prayer. You know the desires of my heart, Lord; grant them, I ask. Yet not my will, Father, but Your will be done.

—*Amen*

ATTITUDE

Therefore, since Christ suffered in his body, arm yourselves also with the same attitude, because he who has suffered in his body is done with sin. As a result, he does not live the rest of his earthly life for evil human desires, but rather for the will of God.

—1 Peter 4:1-2 NIV

A miserable heart means a miserable life; a cheerful heart fills the day with a song.

—Proverbs 15:15 MSG

Your attitude should be the same as that of Christ Jesus: Who, being in very nature God, did not consider equality with God something to be grasped, but made himself nothing, taking the very nature of a servant, being made in human likeness. And being found in appearance as a man, he humbled himself and became obedient to death—even death on a cross!

—Philippians 2:5-8 NIV

We Christia... ...ebrate. God... has risen, and we are the... sometimes, even the most dev... can become discouraged. Aft... world where expectations can be... can be even higher. If you become ... with the direction of your day or your ... turn your thoughts and prayers to God. He is a God of possibility, not negativity. He will help you count your blessings instead of your hardships. And then, with a renewed spirit of optimism and hope, you can thank the Giver of all things good for gifts that are simply too numerous to count.

Some people complain that God put thorns on roses, while others praise Him for putting roses on thorns.

—Anonymous

—A PRAYER—

Dear Lord…I pray for an attitude that is Christlike. Whatever the circumstances I face, whether good or bad, triumphal or tragic, may my response reflect a God-honoring, Christlike attitude of optimism, faith, and love for You.

—Amen

THE BIBLE

For the word of God is quick, and powerful, and sharper than any two-edged sword, piercing even to the dividing asunder of soul and spirit, and of the joints and marrow, and is a discerner of the thoughts and intents of the heart.

—Hebrews 4:12 KJV

Heaven and earth will pass away, but my words will never pass away.

—Matthew 24:35 NIV

Jesus answered, "It is written: 'Man does not live by bread alone, but on every word that comes from the mouth of God.'"

—Matthew 4:4 NIV

Every word of God is flawless; he is a shield to those who take refuge in him.

—Proverbs 30:5 NIV

The words of the LORD are pure words: as silver tried in a furnace of earth.

—Psalm 12:6 KJV

The Bible is a priceless gift, a tool for Christians to use as they share the Good News of their Savior, Christ Jesus. Too many Christians, however, keep their spiritual tool kits tightly closed and out of sight. Jonathan Edwards advised, "Be assiduous in reading the Holy Scriptures. This is the fountain whence all knowledge in divinity must be derived. Therefore let not this treasure lie by you neglected." God's Holy Word is, indeed, a priceless, one-of-a-kind treasure. Handle it with care, but more importantly, handle it every day.

God's Word is a light not only to our path but to our thinking. Place it in your heart today, and you will never walk in darkness.

—*Joni Eareckson Tada*

—A PRAYER—

Dear Lord, the Bible is Your gift to me; thank You. When I stray from Your Holy Word, Father, I suffer. But, when I place Your Word at the very center of my life, I am protected and blessed. Make me a faithful student of Your Word.

—*Amen*

BLESSINGS

For surely, O LORD, you bless the righteous; you surround them with your favor as with a shield.

—*Psalm 5:12 NIV*

I will bless them and the places surrounding my hill. I will send down showers in season; there will be showers of blessings.

—*Ezekiel 34:26 NIV*

I will make you into a great nation and I will bless you; I will make your name great, and you will be a blessing. I will bless those who bless you, and whoever curses you I will curse; and all peoples on earth will be blessed through you.

—*Genesis 12:2-3 NIV*

The Lord is kind and merciful, slow to get angry, full of unfailing love. The Lord is good to everyone. He showers compassion on all his creation.

—*Psalm 145:8-9 NLT*

Every good gift and every perfect gift is from above, and cometh down from the Father of lights.

—*James 1:17 KJV*

$\mathcal{P}$salm 145 makes this promise: "The LORD is gracious and compassionate, slow to anger and rich in love. The LORD is good to all; he has compassion on all he has made" (vv. 8-9 NIV). As God's children, we are blessed beyond measure, but sometimes, as busy women in a demanding world, we are slow to count our gifts and even slower to give thanks to the Giver. Our blessings include life and health, family and friends, freedom and possessions—for starters. And, the gifts we receive from God are multiplied when we share them with others. May we always give thanks to God for our blessings, and may we always demonstrate our gratitude by sharing them.

We do not need to beg Him to bless us; He simply cannot help it.

—*Hannah Whitall Smith*

—A PRAYER—

$\mathcal{T}$oday, Lord, I count my many blessings, beginning with my family. You have cared for me, Lord, and I will give thanks and praise You always. Today, let me share Your gifts with others, just as You first shared them with me.

—*Amen*

CHARACTER

May integrity and uprightness protect me, because my hope is in you.

—Psalm 25:21 NIV

Not only so, but we also rejoice in our sufferings, because we know that suffering produces perseverance; perseverance, character; and character, hope.

—Romans 5:3-4 NIV

In everything set them an example by doing what is good. In your teaching show integrity, seriousness and soundness of speech that cannot be condemned, so that those who oppose you may be ashamed because they have nothing bad to say about us.

—Titus 2:7 NIV

A good name is to be chosen rather than great riches, loving favor rather than silver and gold.

—Proverbs 22:1 NKJV

The integrity of the upright shall guide them....

—Proverbs 11:3 KJV

Wise women understand that character is a crucial building block in the foundation of a well-lived life. Character is built slowly over a lifetime. It is the sum of every right decision, every honest word, every noble thought, and every heartfelt prayer. It is forged on the anvil of honorable work and polished by the twin virtues of generosity and humility. Character is a precious thing—difficult to build, but easy to tear down; godly women value it and protect it at all costs.

Character cannot be developed in ease and quiet. Only through experience of trial and suffering can the soul be strengthened, vision cleared, ambition inspired, and success achieved.

—Helen Keller

—A Prayer—

Lord...You are my Father in Heaven. You search my heart and know me far better than I know myself. Today, I choose to be Your servant and to live according to Your commandments. Empower me to be a person of character and integrity, Lord, and let my words and deeds be a testimony to You.

—Amen

CHEERFULNESS

The cheerful heart has a continual feast.

—*Proverbs 15:15 NIV*

This is the day the LORD has made; let us rejoice and be glad in it.

—*Psalm 118:24 NIV*

A cheerful heart is good medicine....

—*Proverbs 17:22 NIV*

God loves a cheerful giver.

—*2 Corinthians 9:7 NIV*

A cheerful look brings joy to the heart, and good news gives health to the bones.

—*Proverbs 15:30 NIV*

Christian life is a cause for celebration. Christ promises us a life of abundance, wholeness, and joy, but He does not force His joy upon us. We must claim His promises for ourselves, and when we do, Jesus, in turn, fills our spirits with His power and His love. Then, we, as God's children, can share Christ's joy and His message with a world that needs both.

Make each day useful and cheerful and prove that you know the worth of time by employing it well. Then youth will be happy, old age without regret, and life a beautiful success.

—*Louisa May Alcott*

—A Prayer—

Dear Lord, You have given me so many reasons to celebrate. Today, let me choose an attitude of cheerfulness. Let me be a joyful Christian, Lord, quick to smile and slow to anger. And, let me share Your goodness with all whom I meet so that Your love might shine in me and through me.

—*Amen*

CHILDREN

And he took a child, and set him in the midst of them: and when he had taken him in his arms, he said unto them, Whosoever shall receive one of such children in my name, receiveth me; and whosoever shall receive me, receiveth not me, but him that sent me.

—Mark 9:36-37 KJV

Train a child in the way he should go, and when he is old he will not turn from it.

—Proverbs 22:6 NIV

Discipline your son and he will give you peace; he will bring delight to your soul.

—Proverbs 29:17 NIV

Listen, my son, to your father's instruction and do not forsake your mother's teaching.

—Proverbs 1:8 NIV

Children, obey your parents in all things: for this is well-pleasing unto the Lord.

—Colossians 3:20 KJV

*E*ach and every child is a priceless gift from the Father above. And, with the Father's gift comes immense responsibility. As parents, friends of parents, aunts, and grandmothers, we understand the critical importance of raising our children with love, with discipline, and with God.

Children are not so different from kites. Children were created to fly. But, they need wind, the undergirding, and strength that comes from unconditional love, encouragement, and prayer.

—Gigi Graham Tchividjian

—A Prayer—

*H*eavenly Father, when I have the glorious opportunity to care for children, let me love them, care for them, nurture them, teach them, and lead them to You. When I am weary, give me strength. When I am frustrated, give me patience. And, let my words and deeds always demonstrate to Your blessed children the love that I feel for them…and for You.

—Amen

CHRIST'S LOVE

Who will separate us from the love of Christ? Will tribulation, or distress, or persecution, or famine, or nakedness, or peril, or sword? But in all these things we overwhelmingly conquer through Him who loved us.

—Romans 8:35,37 NASB

I am the good shepherd. The good shepherd lays down his life for the sheep.

—John 10:11 NIV

As the Father hath loved me, so have I loved you; continue ye in my love.

—John 15:9 KJV

For I am persuaded, that neither death, nor life, nor angels, nor principalities, nor powers, nor things present, nor things to come, nor height, nor depth, nor any other creature, shall be able to separate us from the love of God, which is in Christ Jesus our Lord.

—Romans 8:38-39 KJV

What does the love of Christ mean to His believers? It changes everything. His love is perfect and steadfast. Even though we are fallible, and wayward, He cares for us still. Even though we have fallen far short of God's commandments, Christ loves us with a power and depth that are beyond our understanding. And, as we accept Christ's love and walk in His footsteps, our lives bear testimony to His power and grace. Yes, Christ's love changes everything; may we invite Him into our hearts so it can then change everything in us.

This hard place in which you perhaps find yourself is the very place in which God is giving you an opportunity to look only to Him, to spend time in prayer, and to learn long-suffering, gentleness, meekness—in short, to learn the depths of the love that Christ Himself has poured out on all of us.

—*Elisabeth Elliot*

—A Prayer—

Dear Jesus...I am humbled by Your love and mercy. You went to Calvary so that I might have eternal life. Thank You, Jesus, for Your priceless gift, and for Your love. You loved me first, Lord, and I will return Your love today and forever.

—*Amen*

CONTENTMENT

But godliness with contentment is great gain. For we brought nothing into the world, and we can take nothing out of it. But if we have food and clothing, we will be content with that.

—1 Timothy 6:6-8 NIV

Let your character be free from the love of money, being content with what you have; for He Himself has said, "I will never desert you, nor will I ever forsake you."

—Hebrews 13:5 NASB

I'm just as happy with little as with much, with much as with little. I've found the recipe for being happy whether full or hungry, hands full or hands empty. Whatever I have, wherever I am, I can make it through anything in the One who makes me who I am.

—Philippians 4:12-13 MSG

Satisfy us in the morning with your unfailing love, that we may sing for joy and be glad all our days.

—Psalm 90:14 NIV

The preoccupation with happiness and contentment is an ever-present theme in the modern world. We are bombarded with messages that tell us where to find peace and pleasure in a world that worships materialism and wealth. But, lasting contentment is not found in material possessions; genuine contentment is a spiritual gift from God to those who trust in Him and follow His commandments. When God dwells at the center of our lives, peace and contentment will belong to us just as surely as we belong to God.

Oh, what a happy soul I am, although I cannot see! I am resolved that in this world, contented I will be.

—Fanny Crosby

—A Prayer—

Dear Father, You are my contentment and my peace. I find protection when I seek Your healing hand; I discover joy when I welcome Your healing Spirit. Let me look to You, Lord, for the peace and contentment that You have offered me through the gift of Your Son.

—Amen

41

COURAGE

Be strong and courageous, and do the work. Do not be afraid or discouraged, for the Lord God, my God, is with you.

—1 Chronicles 28:20 NIV

For God hath not given us the spirit of fear; but of power, and of love, and of a sound mind.

—2 Timothy 1:7 KJV

The Lord is my light and my salvation; whom shall I fear? The Lord is the strength of my life; of whom shall I be afraid?

—Psalm 27:1 KJV

I sought the LORD, and he answered me; he delivered me from all my fears.

—Psalm 34:4 NIV

Be strong and courageous. Do not be terrified; do not be discouraged, for the LORD your God will be with you wherever you go.

—Joshua 1:9 NIV

From time to time, all of us, even the most devout believers, experience fear. When the storm clouds form overhead and we find ourselves in the dark valley of despair, our faith is stretched, sometimes to the breaking point. But, as Christians, we are protected by a loving God and a living Savior. The ultimate battle has already been won at Calvary. We, as believers, can live courageously in the promises of our Lord...and we should.

Courage is the price that life exacts for granting peace. The soul that knows it not knows no release from little things....

—Amelia Earhart

—A Prayer—

Lord, sometimes I face challenges that leave me breathless. When I am fearful, let me lean upon You. Keep me ever mindful, Lord, that You are my God, my strength, and my shield. With You by my side, I have nothing to fear. And, with Your Son Jesus as my Savior, I have received the priceless gift of eternal life. Help me to be a grateful and courageous servant this day and every day.

—Amen

DIFFICULT DAYS

For when the way is rough, your patience has a chance to grow. So let it grow, and don't try to squirm out of your problems.

—James 1:3-4 TLB

A time to weep, and a time to laugh; a time to mourn, and a time to dance....

—Ecclesiastes 3:4 KJV

They do not fear bad news; they confidently trust the Lord to care for them. They are confident and fearless and can face their foes triumphantly.

—Psalm 112:7-8 NLT

I took my troubles to the Lord; I cried out to him and he answered my prayer.

—Psalm 120:1 NLT

We also rejoice in our sufferings, because we know that suffering produces perseverance; perseverance, character; and character, hope.

—Romans 5:3-4 NIV

All of us face those occasional days when the traffic jams and the dog gobbles the homework. But, when we find ourselves overtaken by the minor frustrations of life, we must catch ourselves, take a deep breath, and lift our thoughts upward. Although we are here on earth struggling to rise above the distractions of the day, we need never struggle alone. God is here—eternally and faithfully, with infinite patience and love—and, if we reach out to Him, He will restore perspective and peace to our souls.

As we are reminded through our burden of our utter weakness without Christ, we are given the strength to go on.

—Mary Morrison Suggs

—A Prayer—

Heavenly Father, when I am troubled, You heal me. When I am afraid, You protect me. When I am discouraged, You lift me up. You are my unending source of strength, Lord; let me turn to You when I am weak. In the difficult days of my life, let me trust Your plan and Your will. And whatever my circumstances, Lord, let me always give the thanks and the glory to You.

—Amen

ENCOURAGEMENT

Let the word of Christ dwell in you richly in all wisdom; teaching and admonishing one another in psalms and hymns and spiritual songs, singing with grace in your hearts to the Lord.

—Colossians 3:16 KJV

Let us consider how to stimulate one another to love and good deeds.

—Hebrews 10:24 NASB

But encourage one another day after day, as long as it is still called "Today," so that none of you will be hardened by the deceitfulness of sin.

—Hebrews 3:13 NASB

We urge you, brethren, admonish the unruly, encourage the fainthearted, help the weak, be patient with everyone.

—1 Thessalonians 5:14 NASB

*T*hink…pause…then speak: How wise is the woman who can communicate in this fashion! But all too often, in the rush to have ourselves heard, we speak first and think next…with unfortunate results. Today, seek to encourage all who cross your path. Measure your words carefully. Speak wisely, not impulsively. Your words will bring healing and comfort to a world that needs both.

People, even more than things, have to be restored, renewed, revived, reclaimed and redeemed and redeemed and redeemed.

—*Audrey Hepburn*

—A Prayer—

*L*ord, make me mindful of my words. This world can be a difficult place, and many of Your children are discouraged and afraid. Make me a powerful source of encouragement to those in need, and let my words and deeds be worthy of Your Son, the One who gives me courage and strength, this day and for all eternity.

—*Amen*

ENERGY

Those who hope in the LORD will renew their strength. They will soar on wings like eagles; they will run and not grow weary, they will walk and not be faint.

—Isaiah 40:31 NIV

Never be lacking in zeal, but keep your spiritual fervor, serving the Lord.

—Romans 12:11 NIV

He did it with all his heart, and prospered.

—2 Chronicles 31:21 KJV

And whatsoever ye do, do it heartily.

—Colossians 3:23 KJV

The plans of the diligent lead to profit.

—Proverbs 21:5 NIV

If you're a woman with too many demands and too few hours, don't fret. Instead, focus upon God and upon His love for you. God will give you the strength to do the most important things on today's to-do list…if you ask Him. So ask Him.

When the dream of our heart is one that God has planted there, a strange happiness flows into us. At that moment, all of the spiritual resources of the universe are released to help us. Our praying is then at one with the will of God and becomes a channel for the Creator's purposes for us and our world.

—Catherine Marshall

—A Prayer—

Lord, let me find my strength in You. When I am weary, give me rest. When I feel overwhelmed, let me look to You for my priorities. Let Your power be my power, Lord, and let Your way be my way, today and forever.

—Amen

EVIL

Submit yourselves therefore to God. Resist the devil, and he will flee from you. Draw nigh to God, and he will draw nigh to you.

—James 4:7-8 KJV

Be self-controlled and alert. Your enemy the devil prowls around like a roaring lion looking for someone to devour. Resist him, standing firm in the faith....

—1 Peter 5:8-9 NIV

Be not wise in thine own eyes: fear the LORD, and depart from evil.

—Proverbs 3:7 KJV

Be not overcome of evil, but overcome evil with good.

—Romans 12:21 KJV

He will have no fear of bad news; his heart is steadfast, trusting in the LORD.

—Psalm 112:7 NIV

How hard is it to bump into temptation in today's world? Not very hard. The devil, it seems, is working harder than ever while causing pain and heartache in more ways than ever before. We, as Christians, must be steadfast. Not only must we resist Satan when he confronts us, but we must also avoid those places where Satan can most easily tempt us. As believing Christians, we must beware, and we must earnestly wrap ourselves in the protection of God's Word. When we do, we are secure.

Of two evils, choose neither.

C. H. Spurgeon

—A Prayer—

Dear Lord, strengthen my walk with You. Evil can devour me, and it comes in so many disguises. Sometimes, Father, I need Your help to recognize right from wrong. Your presence in my life enables me to choose truth and to live a life that is pleasing to You. May I always live in Your presence, and may I walk with You today...and forever.

—*Amen*

>>>
FAITH
>>>

Fight the good fight of faith; take hold of the eternal life to which you were called....

—1 Timothy 6:12 NASB

Have faith in the LORD your God and you will be upheld....

—2 Chronicles 20:20 NIV

We live by faith, not by sight.

—2 Corinthians 5:7 NIV

Let us hold fast the profession of our faith without wavering; for he is faithful....

—Hebrews 10:23 KJV

I have fought a good fight, I have finished my course, I have kept the faith.

—2 Timothy 4:7 KJV

The author of Hebrews makes the point clearly and forcefully: the just shall live by faith. When a suffering woman sought healing by merely touching the hem of His cloak, Jesus replied, "Daughter, be of good comfort; thy faith hath made thee whole" (Matthew 9:24 KJV). The message to believers of every generation is clear: live by faith today and every day. If your faith is being tested to the point of breaking, know that Your Savior is near. If you reach out to Him in faith, He will give you peace and heal your broken spirit.

Faith in faith is pointless. Faith in a living, active God moves mountains.

—Beth Moore

—A PRAYER—

Lord, when this world becomes a fearful place, give me faith. When I am filled with uncertainty and doubt, give me faith. In the dark moments, help me to remember that You are always near and that You can overcome any challenge. And, in the joyous moments, keep me mindful that every gift comes from You. In every aspect of my life, Lord, and in every circumstance, give me faith.

—Amen

FAMILY

These should learn first of all to put their religion into practice by caring for their own family....

—1 Timothy 5:4 NIV

Every kingdom divided against itself will be ruined, and every city or household divided against itself will not stand.

—Matthew 12:25 NIV

He who brings trouble on his family will inherit only wind....

—Proverbs 11:29 NIV

Let love and faithfulness never leave you... write them on the tablet of your heart.

—Proverbs 3:3 NIV

No family is perfect, even yours. But, despite the occasional frustrations, disappointments, and hurt feelings of family life, your clan is God's gift to you. That little band of men, women, kids, and babies is a priceless treasure on temporary loan from the Father above. Give thanks to the Giver for the gift of family…and act accordingly.

Money can build or buy a house. Add love to that, and you have a home. Add God to that, and you have a temple. You have "a little colony of the kingdom of heaven."

—*Anne Ortlund*

—A Prayer—

Dear Lord, I am blessed to be part of the family of God where I find love and acceptance. You have also blessed me with my earthly family. May I show the same love and acceptance for my own family that You have shown for me.

—*Amen*

FORGIVENESS

And be ye kind one to another, tenderhearted, forgiving one another, even as God for Christ's sake hath forgiven you.

—Ephesians 4:32 KJV

Whenever you stand praying, forgive, if you have anything against anyone, so that your Father in heaven will also forgive you your transgressions.

—Mark 11:25 NASB

Then came Peter to him, and said, Lord, how oft shall my brother sin against me, and I forgive him? till seven times? Jesus saith unto him, I say not unto thee, Until seven times: but, Until seventy times seven.

—Matthew 18:21-22 KJV

Praise the Lord, I tell myself, and never forget the good things he does for me. He forgives all my sins and heals all my diseases.

—Psalm 103:3 NLT

*C*hrist understood the importance of forgiveness when he commanded, "Love your enemies and pray for those who persecute you." But sometimes, forgiveness is difficult indeed. If you are troubled by some past injustice, read God's Word and remember His commandment to forgive. When you follow that commandment and sincerely forgive those who have hurt you, you'll discover that a heavy burden has been lifted from your shoulders. And, you'll discover that although forgiveness is indeed difficult, with God's help, all things are possible.

Forgiveness is not an emotion. Forgiveness is an act of the will, and the will can function regardless of the temperature of the heart.

—*Corrie ten Boom*

—A Prayer—

*D*ear Lord, when I am bitter, You can change my unforgiving heart. When I am slow to forgive, Your Word reminds me that forgiveness is Your commandment. Let me be Your obedient servant, Lord, and let me forgive others just as You have forgiven me.

—*Amen*

FRIENDS

A friend loves at all times, and a brother is born for adversity.

—Proverbs 17:17 NIV

Greater love has no one than this, that he lay down his life for his friends.

—John 15:13 NIV

Iron sharpeneth iron; so a man sharpeneth the countenance of his friend.

—Proverbs 27:17 KJV

You are my friends if you do what I command. I no longer call you servants, because a servant does not know his master's business. Instead, I have called you friends, for everything that I learned from my Father I have made known to you.

—John 15:14-15 NIV

*L*oyal Christian friendship is ordained by God. Throughout the Bible, we are reminded to love one another, to care for one another, and to treat one another as we wish to be treated. As you journey through the day ahead, remember the important role that Christian friendship plays in God's plans for His kingdom and for your life. Christ promises His followers a life of abundance (John 10:10). May your friends bless you abundantly, and may you do the same for them.

Don't bypass the potential for meaningful friendships just because of differences. Explore them. Embrace them. Love them.

—Luci Swindoll

—A Prayer—

*L*ord, You seek abundance and joy for me and for all Your children. One way that I can share Your joy is through the gift of friendship. Help me to be a loyal friend, Lord. Let me be ready to listen, ready to encourage, and ready to offer a helping hand. Keep me mindful that I am a servant of Your Son Jesus. Let me be a worthy servant, Lord, and a worthy friend. And, may the love of Jesus shine through me today and forever.

—Amen

GENEROSITY

Let us not lose heart in doing good, for in due time we shall reap if we do not grow weary. So then, while we have opportunity, let us do good to all men, and especially to those who are of the household of the faith.

—Galatians 6:9-10 NASB

Freely you have received, freely give.

—Matthew 10:8 NIV

Blessed are the merciful: for they shall obtain mercy.

—Matthew 5:7 KJV

Do not withhold good from those who deserve it, when it is within your power to act.

—Proverbs 3:27 NIV

The good person is generous and lends lavishly....

—Psalm 112:5 MSG

hrist showed His love for us by willingly sacrificing His own life so that we might have eternal life: "But God demonstrates his own love for us in this: While we were still sinners, Christ died for us" (Romans 5:8 NIV). When we walk each day with Jesus—and obey the commandments found in God's Holy Word—we are worthy ambassadors for Him. Just as Christ has been—and will always be—the ultimate friend to His flock, so should we be Christlike in our love and generosity to those in need. When we share the love of Christ, we share a priceless gift.

All my experience of the world teaches me that in ninety-nine cases out of a hundred, the safe and just side of a question is the generous and merciful side.

—Anna Jameson

—A Prayer—

ord, You have been so generous with me; let me be generous with others. Help me to give generously of my time and my possessions as I care for those in need. And, make me a humble giver, Lord, so that all the glory and the praise might be Yours.

—Amen

GIFTS

Now there are varieties of gifts, but the same Spirit. And there are varieties of ministries, and the same Lord.

—*1 Corinthians 12:4-5 NASB*

Do not neglect the spiritual gift that is within you....

—*1 Timothy 4:14 NASB*

Since we have gifts that differ according to the grace given to us, let each exercise them accordingly: if prophecy, according to the proportion of his faith; if service, in his serving; or he who teaches, in his teaching; or he who exhorts, in his exhortation; he who gives, with liberality; he who leads, with diligence; he who shows mercy, with cheerfulness.

—*Romans 12:6-8 NASB*

Every good gift and every perfect gift is from above, and cometh down from the Father of lights.

—*James 1:17 KJV*

All women possess special gifts and talents; you are no exception. But, your gift is no guarantee of success; it must be cultivated and nurtured; otherwise, it will go unused…and God's gift to you will be squandered. Today, accept this challenge: value the talent that God has given you, nourish it, make it grow, and share it with the world. After all, the best way to say "Thank You" for God's gift is to use it.

The Lord has abundantly blessed me all of my life. I'm not trying to pay Him back for all of His wonderful gifts; I just realize that He gave them to me to give away.

—*Lisa Whelchel*

—A Prayer—

Lord, You have given all of us talents, and I am no exception. You have blessed me with a gift—let me discover it, nurture it, and use it to the glory of Your Kingdom. Today, let me be a good and faithful steward, Father, of my talents and my possessions. Let me share my gifts with the world, and let me offer praise to You, the Giver of all things good.

—*Amen*

GOD'S COMMANDMENTS

For this is the love of God, that we keep his commandments....

—1 John 5:3 KJV

Happy are those who fear the Lord. Yes, happy are those who delight in doing what he commands.

—Psalm 112:1 NLT

He that hath my commandments, and keepeth them, he it is that loveth me: and he that loveth me shall be loved of my Father, and I will love him, and will manifest myself to him.

—John 14:21 KJV

He who scorns instruction will pay for it, but he who respects a command is rewarded.

—Proverbs 13:13 NIV

Jesus answered and said unto him, If a man love me, he will keep my words: and my Father will love him, and we will come unto him, and make our abode with him.

—John 14:23 KJV

God has given us a guidebook for living righteously, the Holy Bible. It contains thorough instructions which, if followed, lead to fulfillment, righteousness, and salvation. But, if we choose to ignore God's commandments, the results are as predictable as they are tragic. Let us follow God's commandments, and let us conduct our lives in such a way that we might be shining examples for those who have not yet found Christ.

If men will not be governed by the Ten Commandments, they shall be governed by the ten thousand commandments.

—*G. K. Chesterton*

—A Prayer—

Thank You, Dear Lord, for loving me enough to give me rules to live by. Let me live by Your commandments, and let me lead others to do the same. Let me walk righteously in Your way, Dear Lord, this day and every day.

—*Amen*

GOD'S GRACE

You then, my son, be strong in the grace that is in Christ Jesus.

—*2 Timothy 2:1 NIV*

In Him we have redemption through His blood, the forgiveness of sins, according to the riches of His grace which He made to abound toward us in all wisdom and prudence....

—*Ephesians 1:7-8 NKJV*

For it is by grace you have been saved, through faith—and this not from yourselves, it is the gift of God—not by works, so that no one can boast.

—*Ephesians 2:8-9 NIV*

Let us then approach the throne of grace with confidence, so that we may receive mercy and find grace to help us in our time of need.

—*Hebrews 4:16 NIV*

But He gives more grace. Therefore He says: "God resists the proud, But gives grace to the humble."

—*James 4:6 NKJV*

We have not earned our salvation; it is a gift from God. When we accept Christ as our Savior, we are saved by God's grace. Let us praise God for His gift, and let us share the Good News with all who cross our paths. God's grace is the ultimate gift, and we owe to Him the ultimate in thanksgiving. We demonstrate our thanks by sharing His message and His love.

How beautiful it is to learn that grace isn't fragile, and that in the family of God we can fail and not be a failure.

—*Gloria Gaither*

—A Prayer—

Heavenly Father, accepting Your grace can be hard. Somehow, I feel that I must earn Your love and Your acceptance. Yet, the Bible promises that You love me and save me by Your grace. It is a gift I can only accept and cannot earn. Thank You for Your priceless, everlasting gift.

—*Amen*

God's Love

The unfailing love of the Lord never ends!

—*Lamentations 3:22 NLT*

But God demonstrates his own love for us in this: While we were still sinners, Christ died for us.

—*Romans 5:8 NIV*

For he chose us in him before the creation of the world to be holy and blameless in his sight. In love he predestined us to be adopted as his sons through Jesus Christ, in accordance with his pleasure and will....

—*Ephesians 1:4-5 NIV*

For God so loved the world that he gave his one and only Son, that whoever believes in him shall not perish but have eternal life.

—*John 3:16 NIV*

$\mathcal{G}$od loves you with a depth and breadth that are beyond human understanding. He made you in His own image and gave you salvation through the person of His Son Jesus Christ. And now, precisely because you are a wondrous creation treasured by God, a question presents itself: What will you do in response to God's love? Will you ignore it or embrace it? Will you return it or neglect it? The decision, of course, is yours and yours alone. When you embrace God's love, you are forever changed; accept His love today and forever.

Believing that you are loved will set you free to be who God created you to be. So rest in His love and just be yourself.

—*Lisa Whelchel*

—A Prayer—

$\mathcal{D}$ear Lord, You are love. I love You, Lord, and as I love You more, I am able to love my family and friends more. Let me be Your loving servant, Heavenly Father, today and throughout eternity.

—*Amen*

GOD'S PLAN

It is God who works in you to will and to act according to his good purpose.

—Philippians 2:13 NIV

In his heart a man plans his course, but the Lord determines his steps.

—Proverbs 16:9 NIV

Unless the Lord builds a house, the work of the builders is useless.

—Psalm 127:1 NLT

The Lord says, "I will guide you along the best pathway for your life. I will advise you and watch over you."

—Psalm 32:8 NLT

O the depth of the riches both of the wisdom and knowledge of God! how unsearchable are his judgments, and his ways past finding out! For who hath known the mind of the Lord? or who hath been his counselor?

—Romans 11:33-34 KJV

*G*od has plans for your life, but He won't force you to follow His will. To the contrary, He has given you free will, the ability to make choices and decisions on your own. With the freedom to choose comes the responsibility of living with the consequences of those choices, so choose wisely, study God's Word, and be watchful for His signs. God intends to use you in wonderful, unexpected ways. Find God's plan for your life and follow it.

God has plans—not problems—for our lives. Before she died in the concentration camp in Ravensbruck, my sister Betsie said to me, "Corrie, your whole life has been a training for the work you are doing here in prison—and for the work you will do afterward."

—*Corrie ten Boom*

—A Prayer—

*D*ear Lord, let me choose Your plans. You created me, and You have called me to do Your work here on earth. Today, I choose to seek Your will and to live it, knowing that when I trust in You, I am eternally blessed.

—*Amen*

GOD'S SUPPORT

I am holding you by your right hand—I, the LORD your God. And I say to you, "Do not be afraid. I am here to help you...."

—Isaiah 41:13 NLT

But my God shall supply all your need according to his riches in glory by Christ Jesus.

—Philippians 4:19 KJV

I know the Lord is always with me. I will not be shaken, for he is right beside me.

—Psalm 16:8 NLT

If God is for us, who can be against us?

—Romans 8:31 NIV

Give your burdens to the Lord, and he will take care of you. He will not permit the godly to slip and fall.

—Psalm 55:22 NLT

Women know that life is not always easy. Far from it. But, godly women also know that they are protected by a loving God. In times of trouble, God comforts us; in times of sorrow, He dries our tears. When we are troubled, or weak, or sorrowful, God is as near as our next breath. Let us build our lives on the rock that cannot be shaken…let us trust in God.

The last and greatest lesson that the soul has to learn is the fact that God, and God alone, is enough for all its needs. This is the lesson that all His dealings with us are meant to teach; and this is the crowning discovery of our whole Christian life. God is enough!

—*Hannah Whitall Smith*

—A PRAYER—

Lord…You have promised never to leave me or forsake me. You are always with me, protecting me and encouraging me. Whatever this day may bring, I thank You for Your love and for Your support. Let me lean upon You, Father, this day and forever.

—*Amen*

>>
GOD'S TIMING
>>

Humble yourselves, therefore, under God's mighty hand, that he may lift you up in due time.

—*1 Peter 5:6 NIV*

From one man he made every nation of men, that they should inhabit the whole earth; and he determined the times set for them and the exact places where they should live.

—*Acts 17:26 NIV*

To every thing there is a season, and a time to every purpose under the heaven: A time to be born, and a time to die; a time to plant, and a time to pluck up that which is planted; A time to kill, and a time to heal; a time to break down, and a time to build up; A time to weep, and a time to laugh; a time to mourn, and a time to dance; A time to cast away stones, and a time to gather stones together; a time to embrace, and a time to refrain from embracing; A time to get, and a time to lose; a time to keep, and a time to cast away; A time to rend, and a time to sew; a time to keep silence, and a time to speak; A time to love, and a time to hate; a time of war, and a time of peace.

—*Ecclesiastes 3:1-8 KJV*

We human beings are impatient. We know what we want, and we know exactly when we want it: NOW! But, God knows better. He has created a world that unfolds according to His own timetable, not ours. Let us be patient as we wait for God to reveal the glorious plans that He has for our lives.

He whose attitude towards Christ is correct does indeed ask "in His Name" and receives what he asks for if it is something which does not stand in the way of his salvation. He gets it, however, only when he ought to receive it, for certain things are not refused us, but their granting is delayed to a fitting time.

—*Saint Augustine*

—A Prayer—

Dear Lord...Your timing is seldom my timing, but Your timing is always right for me. You are my Father, and You have a plan for my life that is grander than I can imagine. When I am impatient, remind me that You are never early or late. You are always on time, Lord, so let me trust in You...always.

—*Amen*

THE GOLDEN RULE

Do to others as you would have them do to you.

—*Luke 6:31 NIV*

See that no one pays back evil for evil, but always try to do good to each other and to everyone else.

—*1 Thessalonians 5:15 TLB*

As we have therefore opportunity, let us do good unto all men, especially unto them who are of the household of faith.

—*Galatians 6:10 KJV*

Bear ye one another's burdens, and so fulfil the law of Christ.

—*Galatians 6:2 KJV*

Don't be selfish…. Be humble, thinking of others as better than yourself.

—*Philippians 2:3 TLB*

*T*he words of Luke 6:31 remind us that, as believers in Christ, we are commanded to treat others as we wish to be treated. This commandment is, indeed, the Golden Rule for Christians of every generation. When we weave the thread of kindness into the very fabric of our lives, we give glory to the One who gave His life for us.

Do all the good you can. By all the means you can. In all the ways you can. In all the places you can. At all the times you can. To all the people you can. As long as ever you can.

—John Wesley

—A Prayer—

*D*ear Lord, let me treat others as I wish to be treated. Because I expect kindness, let me be kind. Because I wish to be loved, let me be loving. Because I need forgiveness, let me be merciful. In all things, Lord, let me live by the Golden Rule that is the commandment of Your Son Jesus.

—Amen

GRATITUDE

Therefore, since we receive a kingdom which cannot be shaken, let us show gratitude, by which we may offer to God an acceptable service with reverence and awe....

—Hebrews 12:28 NASB

And let the peace of God rule in your hearts... and be ye thankful.

—Colossians 3:15 KJV

Praise the LORD. Give thanks to the LORD, for he is good; his love endures forever.

—Psalm 106:1 NIV

I will praise the name of God with a song, and will magnify him with thanksgiving.

—Psalm 69:30 KJV

It is good to give thanks to the Lord, to sing praises to the Most High. It is good to proclaim your unfailing love in the morning, your faithfulness in the evening.

—Psalm 92:1-2 NLT

When we were children, we were taught to say "please" and "thank you." And, as adults, we should approach God in the same way. We should offer up our needs to Him in prayer ("Please, Dear Lord...."), and we should graciously give thanks for the gifts He has given us. Let us praise God and thank Him. He is the Giver of all things good.

———

The best way to show my gratitude to God is to accept everything, even my problems, with joy.

—*Mother Teresa*

—A PRAYER—

Dear Lord, I want my attitude to be one of gratitude. You have given me much; when I think of Your grace and goodness, I am humbled and thankful. Today, let me express my thanksgiving, Father, not just through my words but also through my deeds...and may all the glory be Yours.

—*Amen*

GRIEF

I have heard your prayer, I have seen your tears; behold, I will heal you....

—2 Kings 20:5 RSV

Blessed are they that mourn: for they shall be comforted.

—Matthew 5:4 KJV

They that sow in tears shall reap in joy.

—Psalm 126:5 KJV

Weeping may go on all night, but joy comes with the morning.

—Psalm 30:5 NLT

Rejoice with those who rejoice, and weep with those who weep.

—Romans 12:15 NASB

$\mathcal{G}$rief is the price that life periodically extracts from those who live long and love deeply. When we lose a loved one, or when we experience any other profound loss, darkness overwhelms us for a while, and it seems as if we cannot summon the strength to face another day—but, with God's help, we can. During times of heartache, we can turn to God, first for solace and then for renewal. When we do, He comforts us and, in time, He heals us.

We cannot always understand the ways of Almighty God—the crosses which he sends us, the sacrifices which he demands of us. But, if we accept with faith and resignation his holy will—with no looking back to what might have been—we are at peace.

—*Rose Fitzgerald Kennedy*

—A PRAYER—

$\mathcal{L}$ord, You have promised that You will not give me any more than I can bear. You have promised to lift me out of my grief and despair. I thank You, Lord, for sustaining me in my day of sorrow. Restore me, and heal me, and use me as You will.

—*Amen*

HAPPINESS

Happy are those who fear the Lord. Yes, happy are those who delight in doing what he commands.

—*Psalm 112:1 NLT*

Happy is the man that findeth wisdom, and the man that getteth understanding.

—*Proverbs 3:13 KJV*

Delight thyself also in the LORD; and he shall give thee the desires of thine heart.

—*Psalm 37:4 KJV*

How happy are those who can live in your house, always singing your praises. How happy are those who are strong in the Lord....

—*Psalm 84:4-5 NLT*

*O*ur happiness depends less upon our circumstances than upon our thoughts. When we turn our thoughts to God, to His gifts, and to His glorious creation, we experience the joy that God intends for His children. But, when we focus on the negative aspects of life, we suffer needlessly. Today and every day, let us turn our thoughts—and our hearts—to God.

The happiness for which our souls ache is one undisturbed by success or failure, one which will root deeply inside us and give inward relaxation, peace, and contentment, no matter what the surface problems may be. That kind of happiness stands in need of no outward stimulus.

—*Billy Graham*

—A Prayer—

*D*ear Lord...You are my strength and my happiness. I will rejoice in the day that You have made, and I will give thanks for the countless blessings that You have given me. Let me be a joyful Christian, Father, as I share the Good News of Your Son...and let me praise You for all the marvelous things you have done.

—*Amen*

HOPE

The Lord is good to those whose hope is in him, to the one who seeks him; it is good to wait quietly for the salvation of the Lord.

—Lamentations 3:25-26 NIV

Now faith is the substance of things hoped for, the evidence of things not seen.

—Hebrews 11:1 KJV

Happy is he...whose hope is in the LORD his God.

—Psalm 146:5 KJV

But as for me, I will hope continually, and will praise You yet more and more.

—Psalm 71:14 NASB

*E*very woman knows that hope is a perishable commodity. Despite God's promises, despite Christ's love, and despite our countless blessings, we frail humans can still lose hope from time to time. When we do, we need the encouragement of Christian friends, the life-changing power of prayer, and the healing truth of God's Holy Word. If we find ourselves falling into the spiritual traps of worry and discouragement, we should seek the healing touch of Jesus and the encouraging words of fellow Christians. This world can be a place of trials and struggles, but God has promised us peace, joy, and eternal life if we give ourselves to Him.

No other religion, no other philosophy promises new bodies, hearts, and minds. Only in the Gospel of Christ do hurting people find such incredible hope.

—*Joni Eareckson Tada*

—A Prayer—

*T*oday, Dear Lord, I will live in hope. If I become discouraged, I will turn to You. If I grow weary, I will seek strength in You. In every aspect of my life, I will trust You. You are my Father, Lord, and I place my hope and my faith in You.

—*Amen*

JESUS

In the beginning was the Word, and the Word was with God, and the Word was God.... And the Word was made flesh, and dwelt among us, (and we beheld his glory, the glory as of the only begotten of the Father,) full of grace and truth.

—John 1:1,14 KJV

Jesus answered, "I am the way and the truth and the life. No one comes to the Father except through me. If you really knew me, you would know my Father as well. From now on, you do know him and have seen him."

—John 14:6-7 NIV

Jesus Christ the same yesterday, and today, and for ever.

—Hebrews 13:8 KJV

I am the Vine, you are the branches. When you're joined with me and I with you, the relation intimate and organic, the harvest is sure to be abundant.

—John 15:5 MSG

The old familiar hymn begins, "What a friend we have in Jesus…." No truer words were ever penned. Jesus is the sovereign friend and ultimate savior of mankind. Christ showed enduring love for His believers by willingly sacrificing His own life so that we might have eternal life. Let us love Him, praise Him, and share His message of salvation with our neighbors and with the world.

When we are in a situation where Jesus is all we have, we soon discover he is all we really need.

—*Gigi Graham Tchividjian*

—A Prayer—

Thank You, Lord, for Your Son Jesus, the Savior of my life. You loved this world so dearly, Father, that You sent Your Son to die so that we, Your children, might have life eternal. Let me be ever grateful for that priceless gift, and let the love of Jesus be reflected in my words, my thoughts, and my deeds. Let me always count Jesus as my dearest friend, and let me share His transforming message with a world in desperate need of His peace.

—*Amen*

JOY

Let the hearts of those who seek the Lord rejoice. Look to the Lord and his strength; seek his face always.

—1 Chronicles 16:10-11 NIV

Rejoice evermore. Pray without ceasing. In every thing give thanks: for this is the will of God in Christ Jesus concerning you.

—1 Thessalonians 5:16-18 KJV

Rejoice, and be exceeding glad: for great is your reward in heaven....

—Matthew 5:12 KJV

Shout for joy to the LORD, all the earth. Worship the LORD with gladness; come before him with joyful songs.

—Psalm 100:1-2 NIV

So now we can rejoice in our wonderful new relationship with God—all because of what our Lord Jesus Christ has done for us in making us friends of God.

—Romans 5:11 NLT

hrist made it clear to His followers: He intended that His joy would become their joy. And it still holds true today: Christ intends that His believers share His love, His peace, and His joy. Today, let us celebrate our Savior and share His joy with others just as He freely shares His love and His joy with us.

Joy is not gush; joy is not mere jolliness. Joy is perfect acquiescence, acceptance, and rest in God's will, whatever comes.

—*Amy Carmichael*

—A PRAYER—

ord, You have told me to give thanks always and to rejoice in Your marvelous creation. Let me be a joyful Christian, Lord, and let me focus my thoughts upon Your blessings and Your Love. Help me make this day and every day a cause for celebration as I share the Good News of Your Son Jesus.

—*Amen*

JUDGING OTHERS

Judge not, and ye shall not be judged: condemn not, and ye shall not be condemned....

—*Luke 6:37 KJV*

Speak not evil one of another, brethren. He that speaketh evil of his brother, and judgeth his brother, speaketh evil of the law, and judgeth the law....

—*James 4:11 KJV*

Do not judge, or you too will be judged. For in the same way you judge others, you will be judged, and with the measure you use, it will be measured to you.

—*Matthew 7:1 NIV*

Why do you look at the speck of sawdust in your brother's eye and pay no attention to the plank in your own eye? How can you say to your brother, "Let me take the speck out of your eye," when all the time there is a plank in your own eye? You hypocrite, first take the plank out of your own eye, and then you will see clearly to remove the speck from your brother's eye.

—*Matthew 7:3-5 NIV*

We have all fallen short of God's commandments, and He has forgiven us. We, too, must forgive others. And, we must refrain from judging them. As Christian believers, we are warned that to judge others is to invite fearful consequences: to the extent we judge others, so, too, will we be judged by God. Let us refrain from judging others. Instead, let us forgive them and love them in the same way that God has forgiven us.

An individual Christian may see fit to give up all sorts of things for special reasons—marriage, or meat, or beer, or cinema; but the moment he starts saying these things are bad in themselves, or looking down his nose at other people who do use them, he has taken the wrong turn.

—*C. S. Lewis*

—A Prayer—

Lord, sometimes I am quick to judge others. But, You have commanded me not to judge. Keep me mindful, Father, that when I judge others, I am living outside of Your will for my life. You have forgiven me, Lord. Let me forgive others, let me love them, and let me help them...without judging them.

—*Amen*

KINDNESS

And be ye kind one to another, tenderhearted, forgiving one another, even as God for Christ's sake hath forgiven you.

—*Ephesians 4:32 KJV*

O God, you are my God, earnestly I seek you; my soul thirsts for you, my body longs for you, in a dry and weary land where there is no water. I have seen you in the sanctuary and beheld your power and your glory. Because your love is better than life, my lips will glorify you.

—*Psalm 63:1-3 NIV*

Verily I say unto you, Inasmuch as ye have done it unto one of the least of these my brethren, ye have done it unto me.

—*Matthew 25:40 KJV*

Be ye therefore merciful, as your Father also is merciful.

—*Luke 6:36 KJV*

Today, as you consider all the things that Christ has done in your life, honor Him by being a little kinder than necessary. Honor Him by slowing down long enough to say a word of encouragement to someone who needs it. Honor Him by picking up the phone and calling a distant friend…for no reason other than to say, "I'm thinking of you." Honor Christ by following His commandment and sharing His love.

Kind words can be short and easy to speak, but their echoes are truly endless.

—*Mother Teresa*

—A PRAYER—

Heavenly Father, at times this world can become a demanding place, a place where I rush through the day with my eyes focused only on my next step. Slow me down, Lord, and give me wisdom and peace so that I might look beyond my own needs and see the needs of those around me. Today, help me to be generous, compassionate, and understanding. Today, let me spread kind words and deeds to all who cross my path. Today, let the love for Christ shine through me. And let me show kindness to all who need the healing touch of our Master's hand.

—*Amen*

KNOWLEDGE

The fear of the Lord is the beginning of knowledge, but fools despise wisdom and discipline.

—Proverbs 1:7 NIV

By wisdom a house is built, and through understanding it is established; through knowledge its rooms are filled with rare and beautiful treasures.

—Proverbs 24:3-4 NIV

The knowledge of the secrets of the kingdom of heaven has been given to you....

—Matthew 13:11 NIV

It is not good to have zeal without knowledge, nor to be hasty and miss the way.

—Proverbs 19:2 NIV

The lips of the wise spread knowledge; not so the hearts of fools.

—Proverbs 15:7 NIV

If we are to grow as Christians and as women, we need both knowledge and wisdom. Knowledge is found in textbooks. Wisdom, on the other hand, is found in God's Holy Word and in the carefully chosen words of loving parents, family members, and friends. Knowledge is an important building block in a well-lived life, and it pays rich dividends both personally and professionally. But wisdom is even more important because it refashions not only the mind, but also the heart.

The doorstep to the temple of wisdom is a knowledge of our own ignorance.

—*C. H. Spurgeon*

—A Prayer—

Lord, You are my Teacher. Help me to be a student of Your Word and a servant of Your will. Let me live by the truth You reveal, let me trust in the wisdom of Your commandments, and let me teach others the glory of Your ways.

—*Amen*

LAUGHTER

There is a time for everything, and a season for every activity under heaven...a time to weep and a time to laugh, a time to mourn and a time to dance....

—Ecclesiastes 3:1,4 NIV

Clap your hands, all you nations; shout to God with cries of joy.

—Psalm 47:1 NIV

Shout for joy to the LORD, all the earth, burst into jubilant song with music; make music to the LORD with the harp, with the harp and the sound of singing, with trumpets and the blast of the ram's horn—shout for joy before the LORD, the King.

—Psalm 98:4-6 NIV

Nehemiah said, "Go and enjoy choice food and sweet drinks, and send some to those who have nothing prepared. This day is sacred to our Lord. Do not grieve, for the joy of the LORD is your strength."

—Nehemiah 8:10 NIV

*L*aughter is medicine for the soul, but sometimes, amid the stresses of the day, we forget to take our medicine. Instead of viewing our world with a mixture of optimism and humor, we allow worries and distractions to rob us of the joy that God intends for our lives. Today, as you go about your daily activities, approach life with a smile and a chuckle. After all, God created laughter for a reason...and Father indeed knows best. So laugh!

Laughter dulls the sharpest pain and flattens out the greatest stress. To share it is to give a gift of health.

—*Barbara Johnson*

—A Prayer—

*L*ord, when I begin to take myself or my life too seriously, let me laugh. When I rush from place to place, slow me down, Lord, and let me laugh. Put a smile on my face, Dear Lord, and let me share that smile with all who cross my path...and let me laugh.

—*Amen*

LOVING GOD

We love him, because he first loved us.

—1 John 4:19 KJV

Whoever does not love does not know God, because God is love.

—1 John 4:8 NIV

Love the LORD your God with all your heart and with all your soul and with all your strength.

—Deuteronomy 6:5 NIV

I will sing of the LORD'S great love forever; with my mouth I will make your faithfulness known through all generations.

—Psalm 89:1 NIV

And we know that in all things God works for the good of those who love him, who have been called according to his purpose.

—Romans 8:28 NIV

When we worship God with faith and assurance, when we place Him at the absolute center of our lives, we invite His love into our hearts. In turn, we grow to love Him more deeply as we sense His love for us. Saint Augustine wrote, "I love you, Lord, not doubtingly, but with absolute certainty. Your Word beat upon my heart until I fell in love with you, and now the universe and everything in it tells me to love you." Let us pray we, too, will turn our hearts to God, knowing with certainty that He loves us and that we love Him.

Telling the Lord how much you love Him and why is what praise and worship are all about, and it's a perfect anecdote for loneliness because the Bible says that the Lord "inhabits the praise of His people" (Psalm 22:3).

—*Lisa Whelchel*

—A Prayer—

Dear Heavenly Father, You have blessed me with a love that is infinite and eternal. Let me love You, Lord, more and more each day. Make me a loving servant today and throughout eternity. And, let me show my love for You by sharing Your message and Your love with others.

—*Amen*

>>

LOVING OTHERS

>>

And he has given us this command: Whoever loves God must also love his brother.

—1 John 4:21 NIV

Jesus replied, "'Love the Lord your God with all your heart and with all your soul and with all your mind.' This is the first and greatest commandment. And the second is like it: 'Love your neighbor as yourself.' All the Law and the Prophets hang on these two commandments."

—Matthew 22:37-40 NIV

Love one another deeply, from the heart.

—1 Peter 1:22 NIV

And the Lord make you to increase and abound in love one toward another, and toward all men....

—1 Thessalonians 3:12 KJV

Above all, love each other deeply, because love covers over a multitude of sins.

—1 Peter 4:8 NIV

The beautiful words of 1st Corinthians 13 remind us that love is God's commandment: "But now abide faith, hope, love, these three; but the greatest of these is love" (v.13, NASB). Faith is important, of course. So, too, is hope. But, love is more important still. Christ showed His love for us on the cross, and, as Christians, we are called upon to return Christ's love by sharing it. Today, let us spread Christ's love to families, friends, and strangers by word and by deed.

Love is an attribute of God. To love others is evidence of a genuine faith.

—*Kay Arthur*

—A PRAYER—

Father…You have given me love that is beyond human understanding, and I am Your loving servant. May the love that I feel for You be reflected in the compassion that I show toward others. Give me Your eyes to see others as You see them, Lord, and let me show compassion and understanding to those who cross my path this day and every day.

—*Amen*

MIRACLES

God also testified to it [salvation] by signs, wonders and various miracles, and gifts of the Holy Spirit distributed according to his will.

—Hebrews 2:4 NIV

Jesus said to them, "I have shown you many great miracles from the Father."

—John 10:32 NIV

For with God nothing shall be impossible.

—Luke 1:37 KJV

You are the God who performs miracles; you display your power among the peoples.

—Psalm 77:14 NIV

Sometimes, because we are imperfect human beings with limited understanding and limited faith, we place limitations on God. But, God's power has no limitations. God will work miracles in our lives if we trust Him with everything we have and everything we are. When we do, we will experience the miraculous results of His endless love and His awesome power.

We have a God who delights in impossibilities.
—*Andrew Murray*

—A PRAYER—

Dear God, nothing is impossible for You. Your infinite power is beyond human understanding—keep me always mindful of Your strength. When I lose hope, give me faith; when others lose hope, let me tell them of Your glory and Your works. Today, Lord, let me expect the miraculous, and let me trust in You.

—*Amen*

MISTAKES

If we confess our sins, he is faithful and just and will forgive us our sins and purify us from all unrighteousness.

—1 John 1:9 NIV

Therefore if any man be in Christ, he is a new creature: old things are passed away; behold, all things are become new.

—2 Corinthians 5:17 KJV

He who conceals his sins does not prosper, but whoever confesses and renounces them finds mercy.

—Proverbs 28:13 NIV

Have mercy on me, O God, according to your unfailing love; according to your great compassion blot out my transgressions. Wash away all my iniquity and cleanse me from my sin.

—Psalm 51:1-2 NIV

We are imperfect women living in an imperfect world; mistakes are simply part of the price we pay for being here. But, even though mistakes are an inevitable part of life's journey, *repeated mistakes* should not be. When we commit the inevitable blunders of life, we must correct them, learn from them, and pray to God for the wisdom *not* to repeat them. And then, if we are successful, our mistakes become lessons, and our lives become adventures in growth, not stagnation.

If you have made a mistake, even serious mistakes, there is always another chance for you because this thing we call "failure" is not the falling down, but the staying down.

—Mary Pickford

—A PRAYER—

Lord, I know that I am imperfect and that I fail You in many ways. Thank You for Your forgiveness and for Your unconditional love. Show me the error of my ways, Lord, that I might confess my wrongdoing and correct my mistakes. And, let me grow each day in wisdom, in faith, and in my love for You.

—Amen

OBEDIENCE

But if anyone obeys his word, God's love is truly made complete in him. This is how we know we are in him: Whoever claims to live in him must walk as Jesus did.

—*1 John 2:5-6 NIV*

It is the LORD your God you must follow, and him you must revere. Keep his commands and obey him; serve him and hold fast to him.

—*Deuteronomy 13:4 NIV*

If they obey and serve him, they will spend the rest of their days in prosperity and their years in contentment.

—*Job 36:11 NIV*

Jesus replied, "If anyone loves me, he will obey my teaching. My Father will love him, and we will come to him and make our home with him."

—*John 14:23 NIV*

For it is not those who hear the law who are righteous in God's sight, but it is those who obey the law who will be declared righteous.

—*Romans 2:13 NIV*

*T*alking about God is easy; living by His commandments is considerably harder. But, unless we are willing to abide by God's laws, our righteous proclamations ring hollow. How can we best proclaim our love for the Lord? By obeying Him.

God asked both Noah and Joshua to do something unusual and difficult. They did it, and their obedience brought them to deliverance.

—*Mary Morrison Suggs*

—A PRAYER—

*H*eavenly Father, when I turn my thoughts away from You and Your Word, I suffer. But when I obey Your commandments, when I place my faith in You, I am secure. Let me live according to Your commandments. Direct my path far from the temptations and distractions of this world. And, let me discover Your will and follow it, Dear Lord, this day and always.

—*Amen*

OPTIMISM

I can do everything through him that gives me strength.

—Philippians 4:13 NIV

Be of good courage, and he shall strengthen your heart, all ye that hope in the LORD.

—Psalm 31:24 KJV

Make me to hear joy and gladness....

—Psalm 51:8 KJV

Finally, brethren, whatsoever things are true, whatsoever things are honest, whatsoever things are just, whatsoever things are pure, whatsoever things are lovely, whatsoever things are of good report; if there be any virtue, and if there be any praise, think on these things.

—Philippians 4:8 KJV

*E*ven the most devout Christian women fall prey to fear, doubt, and discouragement. But, God has a different plan for our lives. The comforting words of Philippians 4:8 remind us to focus our thoughts on things that are pure and lovely, not upon things that are evil, discouraging, or frustrating. So, the next time you find yourself mired in the pit of pessimism, remember God's Word and redirect your thoughts. This world is God's creation; look for the best in it, and trust Him to take care of the rest.

In spite of everything I still believe that people are really good at heart. I simply can't build up my hopes on a foundation consisting of confusion, misery and death.

—Anne Frank

—A Prayer—

*L*ord, You care for me, You love me, and You have given me the priceless gift of eternal life. Because of You, Lord, I have every reason to live each day with joy and hope. Help me to face this day with a spirit of optimism and thanksgiving so that I may lift the spirits of those I meet just as certainly as I share the Good News of Your Son. And, let me focus my thoughts on You and Your incomparable gifts today and forever.

—Amen

PATIENCE

For when the way is rough, your patience has a chance to grow. So let it grow, and don't try to squirm out of your problems.

—James 1:3-4 TLB

The Lord is wonderfully good to those who wait for him and seek him. So it is good to wait quietly for salvation from the Lord.

—Lamentations 3:25-26 NLT

Wait on the LORD; Be of good courage, and He shall strengthen your heart; Wait, I say, on the LORD!

—Psalm 27:14 NKJV

We also rejoice in our sufferings, because we know that suffering produces perseverance; perseverance, character; and character, hope.

—Romans 5:3-4 NIV

Those who wait upon the Lord, they shall inherit the earth.

—Psalm 37:9 KJV

*P*salm 37:7 commands us to, "Be still before the Lord and wait patiently for Him." But, for most of us, waiting quietly for God is difficult. Why? Because we are fallible human beings, often quick to anger and slow to forgive. Still, God instructs us to be patient in all things, and that's as it should be. After all, think how patient God has been with us.

When I am dealing with an all-powerful, all-knowing God, I, as a mere mortal, must offer my petitions not only with persistence, but also with patience. Someday I'll know why.

—*Ruth Bell Graham*

—A Prayer—

*D*ear Lord, let me live according to Your plan and according to Your timetable. When I am hurried, Lord, slow me down. When I become impatient with others, give me empathy. Today, Lord, let me be a patient Christian, and let me trust in You and in Your master plan.

—*Amen*

PEACE

You will keep in perfect peace him whose mind is steadfast, because he trusts in you.

—Isaiah 26:3 NIV

Be perfect, be of good comfort, be of one mind, live in peace; and the God of love and peace shall be with you.

—2 Corinthians 13:11 KJV

Peace I leave with you, my peace I give unto you: not as the world giveth, give I unto you. Let not your heart be troubled, neither let it be afraid.

—John 14:27 KJV

Blessed are the peacemakers: for they shall be called the children of God.

—Matthew 5:9 KJV

And the peace of God, which transcends all understanding, will guard your hearts and your minds in Christ Jesus.

—Philippians 4:7 NIV

The beautiful words of John 14:27 give us hope: "Peace I leave with you, my peace I give unto you...." Jesus offers us peace, not as the world gives, but as He alone gives. We, as believers, can accept His peace or ignore it. When we accept the peace of Jesus Christ into our hearts, our lives are transformed. Christ's peace is offered freely; it has been paid for in full; it is ours for the asking. So let us ask...and then share.

O God, Thou hast made us for Thyself, and our hearts are restless until they find their rest in Thee.

—Saint Augustine

—A PRAYER—

Dear Lord, when I turn my thoughts and prayers to You, I feel the peace that You intend for my life. But sometimes, Lord, I distance myself from You; sometimes, I am distracted by the busyness of the day or the demands of the moment. When I am worried or anxious, Lord, turn my thoughts back to You. You are the Giver of all things good, Father, and You give me peace when I draw close to You. Help me to trust Your will, to follow Your commands, and to accept Your peace, today and forever.

—Amen

POSSESSIONS

A man's life does not consist in the abundance of his possessions.

—*Luke 12:15 NIV*

Therefore I tell you, do not worry about your life, what you will eat or drink; or about your body, what you will wear. Is not life more important than food, and the body more important than clothes? Look at the birds of the air; they do not sow or reap or store away in barns, and yet your heavenly Father feeds them. Are you not much more valuable than they?

—*Matthew 6:25-26 NIV*

And I will say to my soul, Soul, thou hast much goods laid up for many years; take thine ease, eat, drink, and be merry. But God said unto him, Thou fool, this night thy soul shall be required of thee: then whose shall those things be, which thou hast provided? So is he that layeth up treasure for himself, and is not rich toward God.

—*Luke 12:19-21 KJV*

For where your treasure is, there will your heart be also.

—*Luke 12:34 KJV*

We live in a world that adores material possessions, but on the grand stage of a well-lived life, material possessions should play a rather small role. Of course, we all need basic necessities, but once we meet those needs for ourselves and for our families, the piling up of possessions creates more problems than it solves. Our real riches, of course, are not of this world. We are never really rich until we are rich in spirit.

I have held many things in my hands, and I have lost them all; but whatever I have placed in God's hands, that I still possess.

—*Corrie ten Boom*

—A PRAYER—

Dear Lord…my greatest possession is my relationship with You through Jesus Christ. You have promised that, when I first seek Your kingdom and Your righteousness, You will give me whatever I need. Let me trust You completely, Lord, for my needs, both material and spiritual, this day and always.

—*Amen*

PRAISE

The LORD is my strength and song, and He has become my salvation; He is my God, and I will praise Him....

—*Exodus 15:2 NIV*

Through Him then, let us continually offer up a sacrifice of praise to God, that is, the fruit of lips that give thanks to His name.

—*Hebrews 13:15 NASB*

Praise ye the LORD. O give thanks unto the LORD; for he is good: for his mercy endureth for ever.

—*Psalm 106:1 KJV*

It is good to give thanks to the Lord, to sing praises to the Most High. It is good to proclaim your unfailing love in the morning, your faithfulness in the evening.

—*Psalm 92:1-2 NLT*

In the Hebrew version of the Old Testament, the title of the book of Psalms is translated "hymns of praise," and with good reason. Much of the book is a breathtakingly beautiful celebration of God's power, God's love, and God's creation. The psalmist writes, "Let everything that has breath praise the Lord. Praise the Lord" (150:6). As Christians, we should continually praise God for all that He has done and all that He will do. His works are marvelous, His gifts are beyond understanding, and His love endures forever.

Preoccupy my thoughts with your praise beginning today.

—*Joni Eareckson Tada*

—A Prayer—

Heavenly Father, Your gifts are greater than I can imagine, and Your love for me is greater than I can fathom. May I live each day with thanksgiving in my heart and praise on my lips. Thank You for the gift of Your Son and for the promise of eternal life. Let me share the joyous news of Jesus Christ with a world that needs His healing touch this day and every day.

—*Amen*

>>>

PRAYER

>>>

Do not be anxious about anything, but in everything, by prayer and petition, with thanksgiving, present your requests to God.

—Philippians 4:6 NIV

Watch ye therefore, and pray always....

—Luke 21:36 KJV

If my people who are called by my name, will humble themselves and pray and seek my face and turn from their wicked ways, then will I hear from heaven and will forgive their sin and will heal their land.

—2 Chronicles 7:14 NIV

For the eyes of the Lord are over the righteous, and his ears are open unto their prayers: but the face of the Lord is against them that do evil.

—1 Peter 3:12 KJV

If you believe, you will receive whatever you ask for in prayer.

—Matthew 21:22 NIV

When we weave the habit of prayer into the very fabric of our days, we invite God to become a partner in every aspect of our lives. When we consult God, we benefit from His wisdom, His strength, and His love. Today, instead of turning things over in your mind, turn them over to God in prayer. Instead of worrying about your next decision, decide to let God lead the way. Don't limit your prayers to meals or to bedtime. Pray constantly about things great and small. God is listening, and He wants to hear from you. Now.

Don't be overwhelmed…take it one day and one prayer at a time.

—Stormie Omartian

—A Prayer—

Lord, Your Holy Word commands me to pray without ceasing. When I am discouraged, let me pray. When I am lonely, let me take my sorrows to You. When I grieve, let me take my tears to You, Lord, in prayer. And when I am joyful, let me offer up prayers of thanksgiving. In all things great and small, at all times, whether happy or sad, let me seek Your wisdom and Your Grace…in prayer.

—Amen

RELATIONSHIPS

Thine own friend, and thy father's friend, for-sake not....

—*Proverbs 27:10 KJV*

No man hath seen God at any time. If we love one another, God dwelleth in us....

—*1 John 4:12 KJV*

Love does no harm to its neighbor. Therefore love is the fulfillment of the law.

—*Romans 13:10 NIV*

Let the husband render unto the wife due benevolence: and likewise also the wife unto the husband.

—*1 Corinthians 7:3 KJV*

As we travel along life's road, we build lifelong relationships with a small, dear circle of family and friends. And how best do we build and maintain these relationships? By following the Word of God. Healthy relationships are built upon honesty, compassion, trust, responsible behavior, optimism and sharing. All of these principles are found time and time again in God's Holy Word. When we read God's Word and follow His commandments, we enrich our own lives *and* the lives of those who are closest to us.

Line by line, moment by moment, special times are etched into our memories in the permanent ink of everlasting love in our relationships.

—Gloria Gaither

—A Prayer—

Lord, sometimes this world can become a place of busyness, frustration, and confusion. Slow me down, Lord, that I might see the needs of my family and friends. Today, help me cultivate the important relationships in my life. Let me spread words of thanksgiving and encouragement in honor of Your Son. Today and every day, Father, let my love for Christ be reflected through the love that I share with those close to me.

—Amen

RENEWAL

...inwardly we are being renewed day by day.

—*2 Corinthians 4:16 NIV*

I will give you a new heart and put a new spirit in you....

—*Ezekiel 36:26 NIV*

Remember ye not the former things, neither consider the things of old. Behold, I will do a new thing....

—*Isaiah 43:18-19 KJV*

And be not conformed to this world: but be ye transformed by the renewing of your mind.

—*Romans 12:2 KJV*

Create in me a pure heart, O God, and renew a steadfast spirit within me. Do not cast me from your presence or take your Holy Spirit from me. Restore to me the joy of your salvation and grant me a willing spirit, to sustain me.

—*Psalm 51:10-12 NIV*

Even the most inspired Christian women can, from time to time, find themselves running on empty. The demands of daily life can drain us of our strength and rob us of the joy that is rightfully ours in Christ. Are you tired or troubled? Turn your heart toward God in prayer. Are you weak or worried? Take the time—or, more accurately, *make* the time—to delve deeply into God's Holy Word. Are you spiritually depleted? Call upon fellow believers to support you, and call upon Christ to renew your spirit and your life. When you do, you'll discover that the Creator of the universe stands always ready and always able to create a new sense of wonderment and joy in you.

He is the God of wholeness and restoration.

—*Stormie Omartian*

—A PRAYER—

Father, sometimes I am troubled, and sometimes I grow weary. When I am weak, Lord, give me strength. When I am discouraged, renew me. When I am fearful, let me feel Your healing touch. Let me always trust in Your promises, Lord, and let me draw strength from those promises and from Your unending love.

—*Amen*

RIGHTEOUSNESS

Blessed are those who hunger and thirst for righteousness, for they will be filled.

—*Matthew 5:6 NIV*

But seek first his kingdom and his righteousness, and all these things will be given to you as well. Therefore do not worry about tomorrow, for tomorrow will worry about itself. Each day has enough trouble of its own.

—*Matthew 6:33-34 NIV*

The LORD rewarded me according to my righteousness....

—*Psalm 18:20 KJV*

The righteous shall flourish like the palm tree: he shall grow like a cedar in Lebanon.

—*Psalm 92:12 KJV*

But yield yourselves unto God, as those that are alive from the dead, and your members as instruments of righteousness unto God.

—*Romans 6:13 KJV*

*O*swald Chambers, the author of the classic devotional text *My Utmost For His Highest*, advised, "Never support an experience which does not have God as its source, and faith in God as its result." These words serve as a powerful reminder that, as Christians, we are called to walk with God and to obey His commandments. Today, and every day, may we be examples of righteous living to our friends and our families. Then, may we reap the blessings that God has promised to all those who live according to His will and His Word.

A life lived in God is not lived on the plane of feelings, but of the will.

—Elisabeth Elliot

—A Prayer—

*H*oly, Holy, Holy…You are a Righteous and Holy God who commands that I seek to be holy and righteous. Forgive me when I fall short, Lord, and renew a right spirit within me. Let me serve You and obey the teachings of Your Word. Lead me far from temptation, Father, and guide me in Your will for my life.

—Amen

SAD DAYS

"For my thoughts are not your thoughts, neither are your ways my ways," declares the LORD.... You will go out in joy and be led forth in peace; the mountain and hills will burst into song before you, and all the trees of the field will clap their hands.

—*Isaiah 55:8,12 NIV*

May the God of hope fill you with all joy and peace as you trust in him, so that you may overflow with hope by the power of the Holy Spirit.

—*Romans 15:13 NIV*

For whatsoever is born of God overcometh the world....

—*1 John 5:4 KJV*

We are hard pressed on every side, but not crushed; perplexed but not in despair....

—*2 Corinthians 4:8 NIV*

Then they cried unto the LORD in their trouble, and he saved them out of their distresses.

—*Psalm 107:13 KJV*

When we face the inevitable dark days of life, we must choose how we will respond. Will we allow ourselves to sink even more deeply into our own sadness, or will we do the difficult work of pulling ourselves out? We bring light to the dark days of life by turning first to God, and then to trusted family members and friends. Then, we must go to work solving the problems that confront us. When we do, the clouds will eventually part, and the sun will shine once more upon our souls.

We all go through pain and sorrow, but the presence of God, like a warm, comforting blanket, can shield us and protect us and allow the deep inner joy to surface, even in the most devastating circumstances.

—Barbara Johnson

—A Prayer—

Dear Heavenly Father, on those days when I am troubled, You comfort me if I turn my thoughts and prayers to You. When I am afraid, You protect me. When I am discouraged, You lift me up. You are my unending source of strength, Lord. In every circumstance, let me trust Your plan and Your will for my life.

—Amen

Seeking God

The LORD is good to those whose hope is in him, to the one who seeks him....

—Lamentations 3:25 NIV

Seek the LORD while he may be found; call on him while he is near.

—Isaiah 55:6 NIV

Ask and it will be given to you; seek and you will find; knock and the door will be opened to you. For everyone who asks receives; he who seeks finds; and to him who knocks, the door will be opened.

—Matthew 7:7-8 NIV

I seek you with all my heart; do not let me stray from your commands.

—Psalm 119:10 NIV

But if from there you seek the LORD your God, you will find him if you look for him with all your heart and with all your soul.

—Deuteronomy 4:29 NIV

*W*here is God? He is everywhere you have ever been and everywhere you will ever go. He is with you night and day; He knows your every thought; He hears your every heartbeat. When you earnestly seek Him, you will find Him because He is here, waiting patiently for you to reach out to Him...right here...right now.

God is everything. My focus must be on him, seeking to know him more completely and allowing him full possession of my life.

—*Mary Morrison Suggs*

—A Prayer—

*H*ow comforting it is, Dear Lord, to know that if I seek You, I will find You. You are with me, Father, every step that I take. Let me reach out to You, and let me praise You for revealing Your Word, Your way, and Your love.

—*Amen*

SERVING OTHERS

Therefore, since we receive a kingdom which cannot be shaken, let us show gratitude, by which we may offer to God an acceptable service with reverence and awe....

—Hebrews 12:28 NASB

And he sat down, and called the twelve, and saith unto them, If any man desire to be first, the same shall be last of all, and servant of all.

—Mark 9:35 KJV

Suppose a brother or a sister is without clothes and daily food. If one of you says to him, "Go, I wish you well; keep warm and well fed," but does nothing about his physical needs, what good is it?

—James 2:15-16 NIV

But a Samaritan, as he traveled, came where the man was; and when he saw him, he took pity on him. He went to him and bandaged his wounds, pouring on oil and wine. Then he put the man on his own donkey, took him to an inn and took care of him.

—Luke 10:33-34 NIV

The teachings of Jesus are unambiguous: We achieve greatness through service to others. But, as weak human beings, we sometimes fall short as we seek to puff ourselves up and glorify our own accomplishments. Jesus commands otherwise. If we seek spiritual greatness, we must first become servants.

Christians are like the flowers in a garden: they have upon them the dew of heaven, which, being shaken by the wind, they let fall at each other's roots, whereby they are jointly nourished.

—*John Bunyan*

—**A Prayer**—

Father in heaven…when Jesus humbled Himself and became a servant, He also became an example for His followers. Today, as I serve my family and friends, I do so in the name of Jesus, my Lord and Master. Guide my steps, Father, and let my service be pleasing to You.

—*Amen*

>>>

SHARING

>>>

I will make you into a great nation and I will bless you; I will make your name great, and you will be a blessing. I will bless those who bless you, and whoever curses you I will curse; and all peoples on earth will be blessed through you.

—Genesis 12:2-3 NIV

In everything I did, I showed you that by this kind of hard work we must help the weak, remembering the words the Lord Jesus himself said: "It is more blessed to give than to receive."

—Acts 20:35 NIV

He that hath two coats, let him impart to him that hath none; and he that hath meat, let him do likewise.

—Luke 3:11 KJV

You are the light of the world. A city on a hill cannot be hidden. Neither do people light a lamp and put it under a bowl. Instead they put it on its stand, and it gives light to everyone in the house. In the same way, let your light shine before men, that they may see your good deeds and praise your Father in heaven.

—Matthew 5:14-16 NIV

We live in a "Me first" world that is fast-paced and competitive. However, God instructs us to do otherwise. In God's kingdom, those who proclaim, "Me first," are last. God loves a cheerful, selfless giver. If we seek greatness in God's eyes, we must look our neighbors squarely in the eye and say, "You first." When we do, we will follow in the footsteps of the humble servant who died for our sins: Christ Jesus.

When you cease to contribute, you begin to die.

—*Eleanor Roosevelt*

—A Prayer—

Lord, I know there is no happiness in keeping Your blessings for myself. True joy is found in sharing what I have with others. Make me a generous, loving, humble servant, Dear Lord, as I follow the example of Your Son Jesus.

—*Amen*

SPIRITUAL GROWTH

Whosoever cometh to me, and heareth my sayings, and doeth them, I will show you to whom he is like: he is like a man which built a house, and digged deep, and laid the foundation on a rock: and when the flood arose, the stream beat vehemently upon that house, and could not shake it; for it was founded upon a rock.

—Luke 6:47-48 KJV

When I was a child, I spake as a child, I understood as a child, I thought as a child: but when I became a man, I put away childish things.

—1 Corinthians 13:11 KJV

But grow in the grace and knowledge of our Lord and Savior Jesus Christ.

—2 Peter 3:18 NIV

Therefore let us leave the elementary teachings about Christ and go on to maturity....

—Hebrews 6:1 NIV

He who began a good work in you will carry it on to completion until the day of Christ Jesus.

—Philippians 1:6 NIV

Although you were saved by God's grace in an instant, the process of following Christ is a lifelong journey. Spiritual maturity is gained day by day; it is the inevitable result of placing God permanently at the center of your life. Do you seek to grow as a woman and as a Christian? Then make God the foundation of your day and your life. Read His Word, obey His commandments, praise His works, seek His will, trust His providence, and follow His Son.

As God perfects us, He keeps us protected from the pride that might otherwise develop by veiling, to some extent, our progress in our own eyes. The light of the glory of His presence shines two ways: it sheds light on the knowledge of God so that we can learn to see Him more clearly, but it also sheds light on ourselves so that we can see our own sin more clearly.

—Beth Moore

—A Prayer—

Dear Lord, when I open myself to You, I am blessed. Show me Your way, and deliver me from the painful mistakes that I make when I stray from Your commandments. Let me live according to Your Word and let me grow in my faith every day that I live.

—Amen

135

STRENGTH

He said unto me, My grace is sufficient for thee: for my strength is made perfect in weakness.

—*2 Corinthians 12:9 KJV*

The LORD is my strength and my song....

—*Exodus 15:2 NIV*

Whatever your hand finds to do, do it with all your might....

—*Ecclesiastes 9:10 NIV*

Those who hope in the LORD will renew their strength. They will soar on wings like eagles; they will run and not grow weary, they will walk and not be faint.

—*Isaiah 40:31 NIV*

I can do all things through Him who strengthens me.

—*Philippians 4:13 NASB*

*A*re you faced with mountains that seem impossible to climb? Trust in God and keep climbing. Are you weak or weary? Turn your thoughts and prayers to Him. Remember that God is a never-ending source of power and courage. When you are weary, He gives you strength. When you see no hope, God's Word reminds you of His promises. When you grieve, God will, in time, wipe away your tears. Whatever your circumstances, God will protect you and care for you…if you let Him.

In God's faithfulness lies eternal security.

—Corrie ten Boom

—A Prayer—

*D*ear Lord, sometimes life is difficult. Sometimes, I am worried, weary, or heartbroken. But, when I lift my eyes to You, Father, You strengthen me. When I am weak, You lift me up. Today, I turn to You, Lord, for my strength, for my hope, and my salvation.

—Amen

STRESS

You have allowed me to suffer much hardship, but you will restore me to life again and lift me up from the depths of the earth. You will restore me to even greater honor and comfort me once again.

—Psalm 71:20-21 NLT

For you, O God, tested us; you refined us like silver. You brought us into prison and laid burdens on our backs. You let men ride over our heads; we went through fire and water, but you brought us to a place of abundance.

—Psalm 66:10-12 NIV

When my heart is overwhelmed: lead me to the rock that is higher than I.

—Psalm 61:2 KJV

God, who comforts the downcast, comforted us....

—2 Corinthians 7:6 NIV

*E*very woman knows that stressful days are an inevitable fact of modern life. And how do we deal with the challenges of being a busy female in a demanding, 21st-century world? By turning our days and our lives over to God. Elisabeth Elliot writes, "If my life is surrendered to God, all is well. Let me not grab it back, as though it were in peril in His hand but would be safer in mine!" May we give our lives, our hopes, and our prayers to the Father, and, by doing so, accept His will and His peace.

He treats us as children, and all He asks in return is that we shall treat Him as a Father whom we can trust without anxiety. We must take the child's place of dependence and trust, and we must let Him keep the father's place of care and responsibility.

—*Hannah Whitall Smith*

—A PRAYER—

*H*eavenly Father, You never leave or forsake me. Even when I am troubled by the demands of the day, you are always with me, protecting me and encouraging me. Whatever today may bring, I thank You for Your love and Your strength. Let me lean upon You, Father, this day and forever.

—*Amen*

TESTIMONY

Sanctify the Lord God in your hearts: and be ready always to give an answer to every man that asketh you a reason of the hope that is in you....

—*1 Peter 3:15 KJV*

And I say to you, everyone who confesses Me before men, the Son of Man will confess him also before the angels of God....

—*Luke 12:8 NASB*

Whatever I tell you in the dark, speak in the light; and what you hear in the ear, preach on the housetops.

—*Matthew 10:27 NKJV*

We are therefore Christ's ambassadors, as though God were making his appeal through us. We implore you on Christ's behalf: Be reconciled to God.

—*2 Corinthians 5:20 NIV*

*P*aul shares a message to believers of every generation when he writes, "God has not given us a spirit of timidity" (2 Timothy 1:7). Paul's meaning is clear: When sharing our testimonies, we must be courageous, forthright, and unashamed. We know how Christ has touched our hearts and our lives. Now is the time to share our testimonies with others. Let us preach the Gospel through our words and our deeds.

Dorothy Sayers has said that God underwent three great humiliations in his efforts to rescue the human race. The first was the Incarnation, when he took on the confines of a physical body. The second was the Cross, when he suffered the ignominy of public execution. The third humiliation, Sayers suggested, is the church. In an awesome act of self-denial, God entrusted his reputation to ordinary people.

—*Philip Yancey*

—A Prayer—

*L*ord, the life that I live and the words that I speak bear testimony to my faith. Make me a faithful servant of Your Son, and let my testimony be worthy of You. Let my words be sure and true, Lord, and let my actions point others to You.

—*Amen*

>>>
THANKSGIVING
>>>

Give thanks in all circumstances; for this is God's will for you in Christ Jesus.

—1 Thessalonians 5:18 NIV

Make a joyful noise unto the Lord all ye lands. Serve the Lord with gladness: come before his presence with singing. Know ye that the Lord he is God: it is he that hath made us, and not we ourselves; we are his people and the sheep of his pasture. Enter into his gates with thanksgiving, and into his courts with praise; be thankful unto him and bless his name. For the Lord is good; his mercy is everlasting; and his truth endureth to all generations.

—Psalm 100 KJV

I will thank you, Lord, with all my heart; I will tell of all the marvelous things you have done. I will be filled with joy because of you. I will sing praises to your name, O Most High.

—Psalm 9:1-2 NLT

Let the peace of Christ rule in your hearts, since as members of one body you were called to peace. And be thankful.

—Colossians 3:15 NIV

As Christians, we are blessed beyond measure. God has given us the priceless gifts of eternal love and eternal life. We, in turn, are instructed to approach our Heavenly Father with reverence and thanksgiving. But, as busy women caught in the crush of everyday living, we sometimes fail to pause and thank God for the countless blessings He has bestowed upon us. When we slow down and express our gratitude to Him, we enrich our own lives and the lives of those around us. Thanksgiving should become a habit. God has blessed us beyond measure, and we owe Him everything, including our eternal praise.

God is in control, and therefore in everything I can give thanks, not because of the situation, but because of the One who directs and rules over it.

—*Kay Arthur*

—A PRAYER—

Father, Your gifts are greater than I can imagine. May I live each day with thanksgiving in my heart and praise on my lips. Thank You for the gift of Your Son and for the promise of eternal life. Let me share the joyous news of Jesus Christ, and let my life be a testimony to His love and His grace.

—*Amen*

143

TODEAY

For he says, "In the time of my favor I heard you, and in the day of salvation I helped you." I tell you, now is the time of God's favor, now is the day of salvation.

—2 Corinthians 6:2 NIV

Encourage one another daily, as long as it is Today....

—Hebrews 3:13 NIV

Give your entire attention to what God is doing right now, and don't get worked up about what may or may not happen tomorrow. God will help you deal with whatever hard things come up when the time comes.

—Matthew 6:33-34 MSG

Choose for yourselves this day whom you will serve...as for me and my household, we will serve the LORD.

—Joshua 24:15 NIV

This is the day the LORD has made; let us rejoice and be glad in it.

—Psalm 118:24 NIV

For Christian believers, every day begins and ends with God and His Son. Christ came to this earth to give us abundant life and eternal salvation. We give thanks to our Maker when we treasure each day and use it to the fullest. Today, may we give thanks for this day and for the One who created it.

Yesterday is a cancelled check; tomorrow is a promissory note; today is the only cash you have—so spend it wisely.

—Kay Lyons

—A Prayer—

Help me, Father, to learn from the past but not live in it. And, help me to plan for the future but not to worry about it. This is the day that You have given me, Lord. Let me use it according to Your master plan, and let me give thanks for Your blessings. Enable me to live each moment to the fullest, totally involved in Your will.

—Amen

TRUSTING GOD

Do not let your hearts be troubled. Trust in God; trust also in me. In my Father's house are many rooms; if it were not so, I would have told you. I am going there to prepare a place for you.

—John 14:1-2 NIV

It is better to trust in the LORD than to put confidence in man. It is better to trust in the LORD than to put confidence in princes.

—Psalm 118:8-9 KJV

The LORD is my rock, and my fortress, and my deliverer; my God, my strength, in whom I will trust....

—Psalm 18:2 KJV

Trust the Lord your God with all your heart and lean not on your own understanding; in all your ways acknowledge him, and he will make your paths straight.

—Proverbs 3:5-6 NIV

*T*he journey through life leads us through many peaks and valleys. When we reach the mountaintops, we find it easy to praise God, to trust Him, and to give thanks. But, when we trudge through the dark valleys of bitterness and despair, trusting God is more difficult. The next time you find your courage tested to the limit, lean upon God's promises. When you are worried, anxious, or afraid, call upon Him. Remember that God rules both mountaintops and valleys—with limitless wisdom and love—now and forever.

Either we are adrift in chaos or we are individuals, created, loved, upheld and placed purposefully, exactly where we are. Can you believe that? Can you trust God for that?

—Elisabeth Elliot

—A Prayer—

*L*ord, when I trust in things of this earth, I will be disappointed. But, when I put my faith in You, I am secure. You are my rock and my shield. Upon Your firm foundation I will build my life. When I am worried, Lord, let me trust in You. You will love me and protect me, and You will share Your boundless grace today, tomorrow, and forever.

—Amen

TRUTH

…as we have received mercy, we faint not; but have renounced the hidden things of dishonesty, not walking in craftiness, nor handling the word of God deceitfully; but, by manifestation of the truth, commending ourselves to every man's conscience in the sight of God.

—2 Corinthians 4:1-2 KJV

Therefore laying aside falsehood, speak truth, each one of you, with his neighbor, for we are members of one another.

—Ephesians 4:25 NASB

But when he, the Spirit of truth, comes, he will guide you into all truth….

—John 16:13 NIV

Jesus answered, "I am the way and the truth and the life. No one comes to the Father except through me."

—John 14:6 NIV

And ye shall know the truth, and the truth shall make you free.

—John 8:32 KJV

The words of John 8:32 are familiar and profound. The truth, indeed, will make you free. Truth is God's way: He commands His children to live in truth, and He rewards those who follow His commandment. Jesus is the personification of a perfect, liberating truth that offers salvation to mankind. Do you seek to walk with God? Then you must walk in truth, and you must walk with the Savior.

Those who walk in truth walk in liberty.

—*Beth Moore*

—A PRAYER—

Dear Lord, Jesus said He was the truth, and I believe Him. Father, may Jesus always be the standard for truth in my life so that I might be a worthy example to others and a worthy servant to You.

—*Amen*

WISDOM

Let the word of Christ dwell in you richly in all wisdom; teaching and admonishing one another in psalms and hymns and spiritual songs, singing with grace in your hearts to the Lord.

—Colossians 3:16 KJV

If any of you lacks wisdom, he should ask God, who gives generously to all without finding fault, and it will be given to him.

—James 1:5 NIV

A wise man will hear, and will increase learning; and a man of understanding shall attain unto wise counsels.

—Proverbs 1:5 KJV

For the Lord gives wisdom.... He holds victory in store for the upright....

—Proverbs 2:6-7 NIV

The fear of the LORD is the beginning of wisdom, and knowledge of the Holy One is understanding.

—Proverbs 9:10 NIV

Wisdom is not like a mushroom; it does not spring up overnight. It is, instead, like an oak tree that starts as a tiny acorn, grows into a sapling, and eventually reaches up to the sky, tall and strong. Do you seek wisdom? Then seek it every day of your life. Seek it with consistency and purpose. And, seek it in the right place. That place, of course, is, first and foremost, the Word of God.

Learn as if you were going to live forever. Live as if you were going to die tomorrow.

—*Anonymous*

—A PRAYER—

I seek wisdom, Lord, not as the world gives, but as You give. Lead me in Your ways and teach me from Your Word so that, in time, my wisdom might glorify Your kingdom, Lord, and Your Son.

—*Amen*

THE WORKPLACE

But as for you, be strong and do not give up, for your work will be rewarded.

—*2 Chronicles 15:7 NIV*

Work hard so God can say to you, "Well done." Be a good workman, one who does not need to be ashamed when God examines your work....

—*2 Timothy 2:15 TLB*

Moreover, when God gives any man wealth and possessions, and enables him to enjoy them, to accept his lot and be happy in his work—this is a gift of God.

—*Ecclesiastes 5:19 NIV*

Don't work hard only when your master is watching and then shirk when he isn't looking; work hard and with gladness all the time, as though working for Christ, doing the will of God with all your hearts.

—*Ephesians 6:6-7 TLB*

It has been said that there are no short-cuts to any place worth going. Women agree. Making it in today's competitive workplace is not easy. In fact, it can be very difficult. But, even when the workday is long and the workload is difficult, we must not become discouraged. God did not create us for lives of mediocrity; He created us for far greater things. Earning great things usually requires work and lots of it, which is perfectly fine with God. After all, He knows that we're up to the task, and He has big plans for us.

I seem to have been led, little by little, toward my work; and I believe that the same fact will appear in the life of anyone who will cultivate such powers as God has given him and then go on, bravely, quietly, but persistently, doing such work as comes to his hands.

—*Fanny Crosby*

—A PRAYER—

Father, I seek to be Your faithful servant. When I am tired, give me strength. When I become frustrated, give me patience. When I lose sight of Your purpose for my life, give me a passion for my daily responsibilities, and when I have completed my work, let all the honor and glory be Yours.

—*Amen*

WORRY

Consider the lilies how they grow: they toil not, they spin not; and yet I say unto you, that Solomon in all his glory was not arrayed like one of these. If then God so clothe the grass, which is today in the field, and tomorrow is cast into the oven; how much more will he clothe you, O ye of little faith? And seek not ye what ye shall eat, or what ye shall drink, neither be ye of doubtful mind. For all these things do the nations of the world seek after: and your Father knoweth that ye have need of these things. But rather seek ye the kingdom of God; and all these things shall be added unto you.

—Luke 12:27-31 KJV

Yea, though I walk through the valley of the shadow of death, I will fear no evil: for thou art with me; thy rod and thy staff they comfort me.

—Psalm 23:4 KJV

Trust in him at all times, O people; pour out your hearts to him, for God is our refuge.

—Psalm 62:8 NIV

*I*f you are like most women, it is a simple fact of life: from time to time, you worry. You worry about health, about finances, about safety, about relationships, about family, and about countless other challenges of life, some great and some small. Where is the best place to take your worries? Take them to God. Take your troubles to Him, and your fears, and your sorrows. Seek protection from the One who cannot be moved.

Worry is a cycle of inefficient thoughts whirling around a center of fear.

—*Corrie ten Boom*

—A Prayer—

*F*orgive me, Lord, when I worry. Worry reflects a lack of trust in Your ability to meet my every need. Help me to work, Lord, and not to worry. And, keep me mindful, Father, that nothing, absolutely nothing, will happen this day that You and I cannot handle together.

—*Amen*

WORSHIP

Worship the Lord with gladness. Come before him, singing with joy. Acknowledge that the Lord is God! He made us, and we are his. We are his people, the sheep of his pasture.

—Psalm 100:2-3 NLT

I was glad when they said unto me, Let us go into the house of the LORD.

—Psalm 122:1 KJV

A time is coming and has now come when the true worshipers will worship the Father in spirit and truth, for they are the kind of worshipers the Father seeks. God is spirit, and his worshipers must worship in spirit and in truth.

—John 4:23-24 NIV

Reverence for the Lord is the foundation of true wisdom. The rewards of wisdom come to all who obey him.

—Psalm 111:10 NLT

All the earth shall worship thee, and shall sing unto thee; and shall sing to thy name....

—Psalm 66:4 KJV

When we worship God, either alone or in the company of fellow believers, we are blessed. When we fail to worship God, for whatever reason, we forfeit the spiritual riches that are rightfully ours. Every day provides opportunities to put God where He belongs: at the center of our lives. Let us worship Him, and only Him, today and always.

Worship is a voluntary act of gratitude offered by the saved to the Savior, by the healed to the Healer, and by the delivered to the Deliverer.

Max Lucado

—A PRAYER—

Heavenly Father, let today and every day be a time of worship. Let me worship You, not only with words and deeds, but also with my heart. In the quiet moments of the day, let me praise You and thank You for creating me, loving me, guiding me, and saving me.

—Amen